4—

More Card Manipulations
Series
1-4

More Card Manipulations

Series
1-4

by

JEAN HUGARD

DOVER PUBLICATIONS, INC.
NEW YORK

Published in Canada by General Publishing Company, Ltd., 30 Lesmill Road, Don Mills, Toronto, Ontario.

Published in the United Kingdom by Constable and Company, Ltd.

This Dover edition, first published in 1974, is an unabridged and corrected republication of the series originally published by Max Holden, New York, between 1938 and 1941.

International Standard Book Number: 0-486-23060-0
Library of Congress Catalog Card Number: 74-75264

Manufactured in the United States of America
Dover Publications, Inc.
180 Varick Street
New York, N.Y. 10014

CONTENTS

(Each series contains its own detailed table of contents.)

A Note on the Double Pagination

In the original publication of this book, each of the four series had its separate pagination.

In the Dover edition, the original pagination is retained for Series 1. For Series 2-4 the original page numbers [in square brackets] appear alongside the new running page numbers. All cross-references within the text and all page references on series contents pages are to the original [bracketed] pagination.

More Card Manipulations

SERIES 1

Foreword

The success which has been attained by "Card Manipulations, Numbers I to V." has induced the author and publisher to venture on the production of a second series. The same policy will be continued, viz: the publication of new tricks and improvements on old ones, new and improved sleights and flourishes with unprepared cards only and without apparatus, with the closest attention to the simplest and most practical methods of working. As in the first series there will be no "pipe dreams" and no impractical sleights.

I have to render my most cordial thanks to Mr. Frederick Braue, of Almeda, California; Mr. P. W. Miller, of Susanville, California; Mr. Orville W. Meyer, of Denver, Colorado; and Mr. Jack McMillen, of California, for tricks and sleights they have contributed and for the friendly spirit of cooperation they have shown at all times.

New York.
June 21st, 1938.

MORE CARD MANIPULATIONS
No. 1.

CONTENTS

PART I.

TRICKS

THE THREE MUSKETEERS AND D'ARTAGNAN

EFFECT— The four Jacks, referred to as the Three Musketeers and D'Artagnan, are widely separated in the deck, even by the spectators themselves yet they come together in one packet selected by the audience.

WORKING— 1. From any pack, borrowed for preference, throw out the four Jacks face upwards on the table. Introduce them as the Three Musketeers and D'Artagnan: The Jack of Spades being Athos, the dark, silent leader of the gang; Porthos, the burly ruffian, as ready with a bottle or a club as with a sword, is the Jack of Clubs; Aramias, the dapper ladies' man is the Jack of Hearts; and lastly, the Jack of Diamonds represents D'Artagnan, the canny Breton, with a shrewd eye for the cash or diamonds.

Explain that these four are setting off on a vacation, each going his own way but with a pledge to meet at a rendezvous when ordered to do so by the leader, Athos.

2. While making this introduction, separate three cards at the top of the pack secretly. Take them off with a casual riffle and put them face down on the table without any reference to the number.

Pick up Aramis, the Jack of Hearts, saying he is the first to leave, and put the card face down on the three cards.

3. Secretly separate three more cards at the top of the deck as before, riffle them off and drop them on Aramis, saying nothing about the actual number. Take up Athos, the Jack of Spades, as the next of the Musketeers to leave, and put it face down on top of the pile.

4. Now invite a spectator to cut off a number of cards, say ten or twelve, from the remainder of the deck, and place them on the pile. Then have him pick up either of the remaining Jacks, Porthos or D'Artagnan, and put that card face down on the top of the packet.

5. While this is being done, quietly get three more cards ready at the top of the deck in your left hand, riffle them off and drop them on the pile. Finally let a spectator place the last Jack on the pile also face down. Leave this packet for the moment.

6. Hand the remaining cards to be shuffled, have them put on the table and invite a spectator to divide them into two packets. Then remark casually, "You might as well cut the Jack pile too." Let him do this and COMPLETE this cut. The success of the trick depends upon this but the more offhand you are about it the better.

7. Invite your volunteer assistant to place the Jack pile on top of either of the two packets into which the remaining cards were cut, and then to put the other packet on top of all, thus reassembling the deck. The cards may now be cut as often as the company desires, each cut being completed.

8. Point out how widely separated the Musketeers are and how fairly they have been sent on their travels. Pick up the pack, turn it face up and run rapidly over the faces of the cards to show that this is the case. Spot the Jack of Spades, Athos, and draw it back so that it won't be seen. Separate the hands at that point, showing the cards spread in each hand and, in bringing them together, put the right hand portion under the cards in the left hand. Done casually, this will not be noticed but it amounts to cutting the pack at the Jack of Spades, bringing that card to the top.

9. Deal four hands of four cards thus

2   **3**

1   **4**

The four Musketeers will be together at 1. Invite a spectator to call a number one, two, three or four. Whatever number is called, count accordingly to reach the packet of Jacks on that number. Put this packet aside as being the rendezvous at which the Musketeers are to meet. Give any signal you like, riffle the deck, whistle, snap your fingers, anything you please. Turn the other three hands over and spread the rest of the pack to show that the Musketeers have obeyed.

Finally turn the selected packet face upwards and show that they have arrived at the rendezvous.

THE SHEEP AND THE GOATS

EFFECT— From any deck the red and the black cards are separated into two packets, the black cards being referred to as "sheep" and the red as "goats". A spectator chooses one packet and from it selects one card which is replaced in that packet. These cards are encircled with rubber bands and then placed in an envelope which is sealed and held by a spectator. The other packet is also bound with rubber bands, placed in an envelope and held by a second spectator.

The chosen card vanishes from the first envelope and is found, reversed, in the other envelope, a "goat" amongst the "sheep" or vice versa.

WORKING— 1. With any pack begin by separating the red cards from the black. The easiest and quickest way to do this is to hold the cards upright in the left hand, facing you. Push them off one by one with the left thumb, separating the red cards from the black by alternately raising and lowering the left hand, the right hand remaining stationary. (Fig. 1.) When the last card is reached, seize the upper packet with the right hand, thumb on one side, fingers on the other, and strip the packets apart by a turn of the wrist to the left and downwards.

2. Fan the packets, one in each hand, showing the faces of the cards to the audience and refer to the black cards as being "sheep" and the red cards "goats". Invite a spectator to choose one of the packets, we will suppose that he takes the reds, the "goats". Hand that packet to him and in doing so palm the top card by the One Hand Top Palm. (Card Manipulations No. I, page 2.) Take the other packet in the same hand and add the palmed card to the top (p. 41). Hold the packet then in the left hand. One red card, a "goat", is thus on the top of the black cards, the "sheep"

3. Invite the spectator to shuffle his packet, choose one card (always refer to it as a "goat") and hand it to you face down. Take the card in the right hand and, saying to the spectator, "Remember you have chosen a red card, a "goat", and not one of these black cards, the "sheep", make a gesture with the right hand towards the packet in your left hand and top change the chosen card for the red card you have just added to it. (See Top Change, page 42). Lay the substitute card face down on the table.

4. Secretly sight the index of the chosen card (Card Manipulations No. V. p. 137) and slip the bottom card on top of it. Or, if preferred, do this by an overhand shuffle thus: Under cut about half the packet, run one card, injog the next and shuffle off. Form a break at the jogged card, shuffle to the break and throw the remaining cards on top. The chosen card will now be the second card from the top.

5. "Remember", you say, "these cards, the black cards, are the 'sheep'. I will show them to you again." Turn the top card face up and, in so doing push the next card a little over the deck, enabling you to square it with the reversed card, and hold the two as one card by the

lower index corner between the tips of the right thumb above and the first and second fingers below. Hold the right hand rigid and turn the cards in the left hand face upwards with the left thumb. Fig. 2. Spread them on the card(s) in the right hand, showing the faces "All black, that is, all 'sheep,'" you say. Square the cards, still face up, cut at about the middle and turn the packet face downwards.

6. Place two rubber bands around the packet, lengthwise and sideways, insert them in an envelpe, seal it and hand it to the spectator who chose the card. Take the red packet, the "goats," from him and hold it in the left hand.

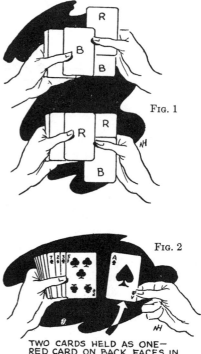

Fig. 1

Fig. 2

7. Lift the substitute card from the table with its face towards yourself and call it by the name of the chosen card which you sighted, saying, "This is your card, the......of ..... ?" On the reply "Yes", push the card at once, without showing the face, into the middle of the packet in your left hand.

8. Place rubber bands around this packet, insert it in an envelope, seal it and give it to a second spectator to hold.

The trick is now done, it only remains to finish it off with appropriate patter. "One of the 'goat's,'" you continue, "contracted a fatal affection for the 's h e e p' and, no matter how he was penned up, always managed to get free and join them. I wouldn't be surprised if you have chosen that very one. What did you say your card was? Oh, yes, the .... of ......" Address the

TWO CARDS HELD AS ONE—
RED CARD ON BACK FACES IN
OPPOSITE DIRECTION

second spectator, "You have the red cards, the 'goats,' still penned up? The envelope is intact? Very well, please open it and take the 'goats' out. The ropes, I mean the rubber bands, are still around them each way? Just run through the cards and see if the...... of ...... is still with the other 'goats'. Not there? I thought not."

Turn to the first spectator, "How is your flock of 'sheep'? Still penned securely? Ropes intact? Just see if that 'goat' of yours, the...... of...... has managed to get amongst the 'sheep'." He finds the card in the packet reversed.

You add, "I think the explanation of the mystery is that that 'goat' is a bit of a 'black sheep' himself"

SNAP!!!
A Quick Trick

EFFECT— A card is freely chosen by a spectator from a thoroughly shuffled deck. The card is noted, returned and the pack again shuffled. The performer spreads the cards in a wide fan, using the reverse method, the fan presenting a blank face. At command the chosen card suddenly springs up into view in the middle of the fan.

METHOD— 1. After having the deck shuffled by a spectator, invite him to choose a card, note what it is and return it to the deck.

2. Control the card by whatever pass, or pass substitute you prefer, bringing it to the top and at once proceed to a false shuffle.

Note here that there is a marked tendency amongst card men to overdo this shuffling by unnecessarily prolonging it and by introducing various flourishes. If it is your object to show the spectators how smart you are, by all means use all the flourishes and quick moves that you can. If, however, you wish to obtain a magical effect, an easy natural overhand shuffle, first bringing the chosen card next to the bottom, then back again to the top, followed by a riffle shuffle which leaves an indifferent card, above it and, finally, the Erdnase blind cut disposing of the indifferent card, will afford ample evidence to the spectators that the chosen card is lost amongst the others.

3. Make the double lift to show that the selected card is not on the top and turn the two cards face down again. Turn the deck face up and call attention to the bottom card by asking the spectator if it is his card. The answer being "No," reverse that card bringing it back outwards, the rest of the cards being face outwards in your left hand.

4. With the pack in this position, face outwards, execute the reverse fan flourish. Owing to the reversal of the bottom card neither the faces nor the indexes of any cards will be visible. Stand with your right side to the front and hold the fan of cards with its blank side squarely to the front.

5. When the right hand has completed the fan, bring it back to the starting point, the thumb on the face of the fan, the fingers on the back and, under pretense of adjusting the cards more evenly, separate the upper end of the chosen card slightly from the others, bend it back and

downwards and, with the help of the left fingers, carry it behind the cards to the middle of the fan. Place the tip of the left third or fourth finger on the end of the chosen card, holding it bent back almost double and, with the other left fingers, push the card upwards about an inch and a half.

6. Continue the pretended adjustment of the edge of the fan for a moment or two, then point to the cards with the right hand and ask the spectator if he can see his card amongst the others. The answer, naturally is "No." Have him name his card and instantly release the upper end of the bent card from the left finger. The selected card at once springs up into view at the top of the fan of cards with an audible snap.

Although the description is necessarily long, the trick will be found to be a very quick and surprising one. It is a favorite trick of Dr. Jack Daley, of New York, who executes it to perfection. He makes another very amusing use of the same idea. Making an ordinary fan with the deck he proffers it to a spectator with the request that he draw a card. The moment before the victim's fingers reach the cards, Dr. Daley releases the end of the bottom card which he had pulled around to the middle as in the Snap trick. It appears that a card has sprung out spontaneously to meet the spectator's hand.

This idea makes an excellent opening for the Ambitious Card trick. After letting the card spring into the spectator's hand, apologise, remarking that that particular card is always giving trouble, and push the card into the middle of the pack. A moment later show it on the top of the deck, then continue with whatever routine you have adopted for the Ambitious Card Trick.

CRIME CLUB SELECTION
A Novel Card Transposition
DR. H. WALTER GROTE

EFFECT— A freely chosen, initialed card is sealed by a spectator in an unprepared envelope and caused to change places with another initialed card in the pack. Any borrowed pack may be used and there are no duplicates, no forces, no prepared envelopes and no envelope switch.

REQUIREMENTS— A borrowed deck, an unprepared party envelope, a pair of scissors, a small pellet of diachylon or magician's wax and a glass.

PATTER SUGGESTION AND EXECUTION

Ladies and Gentlemen,

Hardly a day passes without the headlines of your favorite paper proclaiming the perpetration of some major crime by one of the nation's public enemies. Time and again it has been proven that 'Crime does not pay', but daily Mr. Edgar J. Hoover's department is called upon to match wits with some new cunning master mind of crime. To give you an idea of the resourcefulness of some of the criminals, we will enact the exploits and capture of our own public enemy No. 1.

Now let us suppose that the search has been narrowed down to fifty-three known suspects (PICK UP THE CARDS) and this gentleman, our ablest detective, knows who the real culprit is and has been ordered to make the arrest. Kindly remove any one of the Jacks you may fancy as the criminal. (HAND THE PACK TO A SPECTATOR.)

Now that the arrest has been made, the prisoner is, of course, immediately fingerprinted for future identification. (TAKE THE PACK, HAND THE SPECTATOR A PENCIL AND ASK HIM TO WRITE HIS INITIALS ACROSS THE FACE OF THE CARD. THEN TURN TO ANOTHER SPECTATOR). Valuable evidence may be obtained from the gangster's moll, therefore we shall arrest her too. Will you take out any Queen you may fancy and will you also write your initials across the face of your card? (TAKE PACK BACK AS SPECTATOR WRITES ON CARD).

Now it seems that there is not sufficient evidence against the 'lady' to hold her and we are forced to release her. Will you kindly replace your card in the deck? (CUT THE PACK AND COLLECT THE CARD.) However, we shall place a man to shadow her. (PLACE A KING REVERSED ON TOP OF THIS COLLECTED CARD, CLOSE THE CUT AND MAKE THE PASS, BRINGING THE REVERSED KING TO THE BOTTOM AND THE SELECTED QUEEN TO THE TOP.) This puts her back in circulation but our trusty Hawkshaw, I hope, will keep a close watch on her.

Gumshoe

Now in the case of the arch criminal we will call the patrol wagon (PRODUCE AN EMPTY ENVELOPE) and lock him up in there to have him transported to the Tombs. (HAVE THE SPECTATOR INSERT HIS CARD IN THE ENVELOPE FACE DOWNWARDS, SEAL THE ENVELOPE AND INITIAL IT ON THE FACE. WHILE HE IS DOING THIS SECURE THE PELLET OF DIACHYLON OR WAX AND PRESS IT ON THE TOP CARD, THE SECOND SELECTION. WHEN THE ENVELOPE IS SEALED AND INITIALLED, HOLD IT UP, TURNING IT FROM ALL ANGLES.) Not much chance of an escape is there? (FROWN AND MAKE BELIEVE YOU HEAR SOME NOISE FROM THE INSIDE OF THE ENVELOPE.) Ha, he is complaining, says you can't put him in gaol. (LOOK AT THE SPECTATOR AS YOU SAY THIS AND AT THE SAME TIME CASUALLY LOWER THE ENVELOPE ON TOP OF THE DECK ON THE PALM OF YOUR LEFT HAND. PRESS ENVELOPE FIRMLY WITH LEFT THUMB ON TOP OF DIACHYLON, THEREBY AFFIXING THE TOP CARD TO BACK. WITHOUT HESITATION REMOVE ENVELOPE (AND CARD) HOLDING ITS BACK AWAY FROM THE AUDIENCE WHILE YOU WALK TO YOUR TABLE. PLACE ENVELOPE UPRIGHT LEANING AGAINST A GLASS AND THE PACK ON THE TABLE BESIDE THE GLASS.)

Now the prisoner has arrived at the gaol (POINT TO GLASS) we shall unlock the door, (PICK UP THE SCISSORS) to transfer our catch to the solitary confinement of this modern sunshine cell. (CUT OPEN THE END OF THE ENVELOPE, LAY THE SCISSORS ASIDE AND LOOK INTO THE OPENING.) Hey, you, out with you. Come on now, make it snappy. I believe there is something wrong here. (REACH INTO THE ENVELOPE WITH THE TWO RIGHT MIDDLE FINGERS, RIGHT THUMB ON THE BACK. DRAW FORTH THE TWO CARDS AS ONE, USING THE LEFT LITTLE FINGER, LEFT INDEX FINGER AND LEFT THUMB TO REGISTER THEM PROPERLY DURING THE MOVEMENT. THIS SOUNDS COMPLICATED BUT A TRIAL WILL READILY CONVINCE YOU OF THE NATURALNESS OF THIS PROCEDURE. THE BACK(S) OF CARD(S) ARE TOWARDS THE AUDIENCE WHEN BEING DRAWN FROM ENVELOPE. NOW LOOK AT THE CARDS IN A DUMBFOUNDED MANNER AND THEN TURN THE FACE OF BOTTOM CARD TOWARDS AUDIENCE. Sir, this was the prisoner you locked up to be delivered to the gaol? Shades of Houdini! this is a woman, in fact it is the gangster's moll with whom the rascal has changed places!!

Well, she is an accessory after the fact and we will lock her up immediately. (PALM OFF THE TOP CARD AND PLACE 'MOLL' INTO THE GLASS FACING THE AUDIENCE. WITH THE RIGHT HAND PICK UP THE PACK DEPOSITING THE PALMED CARD ON TOP.) Well, I wonder what our dumb detective was doing all this time. I think he ought to be demoted for letting the girl get away from him. (MAKE THE PASS BRINGING THE TOP AND REVERSED BOTTOM CARD TOGETHER SOMEWHERE IN THE MIDDLE. FAN PACK UNTIL YOU EXPOSE THE REVERSED CARD. CUT HERE AND PLACE THE CARDS ABOVE THE DETECTIVE BEHIND THE REST.) AH! Here he is still parked in front of her apartment. Well, what have you to say for yourself? Eh? He says the girl got away from him but he nailed the big shot when he tried to get into the apartment. And so he has!!! (TURN THE NEXT CARD FACE UP). You may compare the fingerprints. I am sure you will find they check bringing to an end another checkered career. (HAND THE CARD TO THE SPECTATOR WHO INITIALLED IT, ALSO THE CARD IN THE GLASS TO THE SECOND SPECTATOR.)

INFALLIBLE PREDICTION
AUDLEY V. WALSH and HAL HABER

EFFECT— The performer writes a prediction, folds the paper and hands it to a spectator to put in his own pocket. The latter then shuffles a deck of cards, which may be his own, and lays out four cards, taken by himself, face upwards. The spots on these four cards are added together and he counts down in the pack to the total thus arrived at and lays the card that happens to be at that number aside face down. He takes out the prediction and reads the name of the card written there, the card he himself laid aside is turned up, it is the very card. The spectator shuffles the pack at the beginning and the performer does not touch the cards.

REQUISITES— A full deck of 52 cards, a slip of paper and pencil.

WORKING— The pack to be used must be a complete deck of 52 cards and from this you secretly palm two cards and pocket them. The spectator therefore gets 50 cards only but naturally has no suspicion that the deck is not complete. You proceed then as follows:

1. Ask the spectator to first thoroughly shuffle the cards. As he finishes the shuffle get a peek at the bottom card. If you fail to get the card then tell him to square the deck and make a motion of tapping the cards on the table which will bring the bottom card to your view. Announce that you will make a prediction, take the slip

of paper and write the name of the card you have just sighted, fold the slip without allowing anyone to see the writing and hand it to the spectator to place in his pocket.

2. Instruct the spectator to count off ten cards and lay the remainder on the table. Next tell him to shuffle the ten cards and lay four cards face upwards in a row on the table, and place the remainder of the deck on top of the six cards left over.

3. Pointing out that from first to last you do not touch the cards, you instruct him to deal cards from the top of the deck, counting each card as one, onto each of the four face up cards, to make piles totalling ten, beginning with the spot value of each card. For example, suppose the first card of the row is a four spot, he will have to deal six cards on it to make a total of ten required. Court cards may be counted as ten or he may fix an arbitrary value if he wishes.

4. This done tell the spectator to add together the values of the four face up cards, we will suppose that the total comes to 23, he is then to deal from the top of the pack until he reaches that number and put out the twenty-third card face down on the table.

5. Invite him to take your prediction from his pocket and read it aloud. He does so then turns over the card just arrived at which proves to be the very card you predicted before the experiment began.

To make the trick still more puzzling it may be repeated, varying the method to throw the spectators still further off the track.

Again you sight the bottom card after the shuffle and make the prediction as before. This time, however, you have the spectator count off 20 cards and from these place three only face up. Then you follow exactly the same procedure as before and get the same result.

Finally you have only to seize any favorable opportunity of returning the two cards stolen to the deck and it will be impossible for anyone to duplicate the effect.

THE CONTINUOUS SPELLING TRICK
JACK McMILLAN

Using any deck of cards, preferably a borrowed one, let a spectator shuffle it and, on taking it back, secretly sight the top card. Announce that you have merely to name a card and it will at once place itself automatically in position to be spelled out.

While talking execute an overhand shuffle thus: Run twelve cards, injog the next and shuffle off. Form a break at the injog, shuffle to the break and throw the remaining cards on top. The card you sighted will now be the twelfth card and you proceed to spell it in such a way that it turns up on the last letter. To do this requires just a little thought but practice makes it come easy.

The whole attention of the spectators will be directed to the last card of the spelling, giving you ample opportunity to sight the top card of those remaining in the left hand. An easy way is to turn the left hand over in the action of pointing to the card just turned face up, push the side of the top card, buckling it slightly and sight the top index. Fig. 1. (Card Manipulations, No. V. p. 136).

Pick up the cards dealt off, first turning the card just spelled face down, and add them to the top of the pack.  The new card sighted will be the thirteenth. False shuffle and make the Erdnase blind cut No. 1. the top losing one card. Fig. 2. Name the new card and proceed to spell it, using twelve letters as before.

Fig. 1

It will happen at times that the card will spell quite naturally with thirteen letters, for example the three, seven, eight and Queen of Hearts and Spades, in which case omit the false cut.

Fig. 2

The trick can be continued ad lib. but under ordinary circumstances three times will be ample proof of your assertion.

THE BURGLARS
O. W. MEYER

This trick has had many versions, one of which appears in Card Manipulations No. 1. My own method, which follows, has two points which will appeal to the average magician— simplicity of method and a completely unexpected climax.

Explaining that you will use a King to represent a detective and three Jacks as three burglars, remove a King and three Jacks from the deck and place the King face up on the table, the Jacks faces downwards. We will suppose that you have taken the two black Jacks and one red one, the red one must be put between the other two. While you search for these cards, however, you take opportunity to arrange the remaining Kings and Jack in the following manner:

bring one of the Kings to the back, or top of the deck, and the other two Kings to the bottom with the second red Jack between them.

Do all this with the deck facing you and it is well to deliberately MISS one of the Jacks or the King until you have the cards properly arranged. Then "find" the remaining card, place it on the table and proceed. The position now is this, on the table is a King face upwards, two black Jacks with a red Jack between them face downwards; the deck has a King on the top and on the bottom King-red Jack-King. Turn the deck face down and hold it in the left hand, being careful not to let anyone see that there is a King on the bottom.

Now tell the story of three burglars, pick up the three face down Jacks, fan them, showing them casually and replace them face downwards. You relate how "one burglar goes in the front way" and you place a black Jack on the bottom of the pack, thus covering the King, and immediately turn the pack up showing the Jack. "One burglar crawls in through a window", so you pick up the next Jack, the red one, and thrust it into the center of the deck. "The last burglar goes in through the back door" so you show the remaining black Jack and place it on the top of the pack. "The detective, however, arrives in the nick of time and rushes in through the front door", place the King face up on the bottom of the deck.

"A terrific fight ensues," here you cut the deck, "but the detective is victorious, for the commotion has attracted the attention of other officers and upon investigating we find that the three burglars have been completely surrounded by the detectives."

Fan the deck and show the four Kings with the Jacks between them. This unexpected appearance of the three additional Kings will come as a complete surprise.

THE MAGIC THRUST
O. W. MEYER

The effect is that a spectator himself locates a previously selected card, while holding the deck behind his back.

From any deck, which has been shuffled by a spectator, let a card be freely selected and noted. Have it replaced and bring it next to the bottom by whatever method you use, and false shuffle, leaving it in that position. Now let a second spectator draw a card, take it and show it, asking if it is the card first chosen. On being assured that it is not, lay it face up on the top of the deck.

Invite the spectator who drew the first card to stand on your left side, facing the audience with you. Tell him he is to hold his hands behind his back and that you will place the pack in his hands, then he is to take off the reversed card from the top and thrust it into the middle of the deck.

As you put the cards behind his back, simply turn the whole deck over. He takes the top card, which is face up, the same as all the rest except one, and pushes it into the middle of the pack where it is simply lost. Next instruct him to cut about one-fourth of the pack from the top to the bottom. This, you remind him, simply has the effect of bringing the reversed card he thrust in the center, a little nearer to the top of the pack.

Now you can take the cards from him, bringing them into sight once more, but, under cover of his back, turn the whole pack over again bringing it right side up. Or hand him a handkerchief and ask him to wrap the cards up in it and then hand the package to you.

Examination of the cards reveals the reversed card FACE TO FACE with the one he chose. The effect is that he himself has discovered his own card.

This improved method eliminates the necessity for the Charlier pass as in a previous version. When you place the pack behind the spectator's back, hold it by the thumb and finger tips only and you will baffle the magus who may be expecting the Charlier pass to be used. You will find this an excellent impromptu feat.

THE TWO JOKERS
P. W. MILLER

EFFECT: An otherwise ordinary deck is shown to have two Jokers. These are removed and laid on the table. The deck is shuffled and a spectator is invited to make a free choice of a card which is shown to everyone but the performer who turns away. The spectator then places the two Jokers in different places in the pack and it is thoroughly shuffled. The deck is then covered with a handkerchief, the spectator thrusts his chosen card face upward into it and squares the deck.

The performer very openly spreads the cards ribbonwise on the table. The two cards, one on each side of the chosen reversed card, are pushed forward. The spectator himself turns them face up. They are the two Jokers.

REQUIREMENTS— Three decks, two ordinary ones, from one of which the Joker has been removed and placed in the other, and a forcing pack consisting of Jokers only, all three with the same pattern on the backs. The ordinary, Jokerless pack is placed in your left outside coat pocket, the forcing deck in the left upper vest pocket and the ordinary deck with the two Jokers is placed on the table.

WORKING— 1. Remove the two Jokers from the pack and place them on the table. Have the deck shuffled by a spectator and then allow him to choose a card freely. Invite him to show the card to everyone as you turn away.

2. Turn your back, drop the deck into your breast pocket and take the forcing deck from the vest pocket, being careful not to move the elbows (or make any other exchange that you may prefer). Turn around and have the two Jokers placed in the pack in different places, then shuffle thoroughly. You may even allow a spectator to shuffle if you can rely on his using an overhand shuffle.

3. Lay the deck on the table and cover it with a handkerchief. Invite the spectator to thrust his chosen card, face upwards, into the deck under the handkerchief.

4. Assert that the two Jokers will at once join the chosen card and place themselves one on each side of it. Remove the handkerchief and spread the cards ribbonwise on the table. Push forward the reversed card together with the one above it and the one below. Gather up the remainder of the cards and hold them in the left hand.

5. Invite the spectator to turn up the two face down cards. They are the Jokers.

As he does this stand with your right side to the front, drop the pack from your left hand into the left coat pocket and take the ordinary deck which is minus the Jokers.

Bridge decks nowadays generally have two Jokers in each deck and are therefore the best to use for the trick.

THE LADIES' LOOKINGGLASS

A New Version

EFFECT— Four spectators each choose a pair of cards, they are replaced and the deck shuffled. Three of the pairs appear at command, one card on the top, the other on the bottom of the deck. Throwing the pack in the air the magician catches the last pair at his finger tips.

WORKING— Any deck of cards may be used. Invite a spectator to shuffle the cards and retain one card. Take the pack, spread it with the faces towards him and have him pick out a second card of same value, at the same time turn your head away so that there may be no suspicion of your getting a glimpse of it. Let him replace the two cards together in the deck, pass them to the top, execute a false shuffle, then palm the two cards in your right hand and hold the deck in that hand.

Pass the pack to a spectator on your left, inviting him also to shuffle and pick out two cards of the same value. As he does this thrust both hands in your trousers' pockets as you make some remark about the way he shuffles and leave the palmed cards in the right hand pocket. When he has chosen two cards, take the pack from him. Have this second pair replaced, both cards together, and pass them to the top. False shuffle retaining the two cards on the top thus: Under cut about half the cards, injog one and shuffle off. Make a break at the jogged card, shuffle to the break and throw the remaining cards on top.

Go to a third person and have him freely select a card. Spread the faces of the cards before him and invite him to take a second card of the same value as the card he has selected, turning your head away as before. As he notes his cards, shuffle again by under cutting about half the cards, jogging one card and shuffling off. Cut at the jogged card and have the third pair returned on top of the second pair. By means of the pass, or pass substitute, bring the two pairs to the top and make a false shuffle retaining them there.

Repeat exactly the same process with a fourth spectator so that the pairs of cards drawn by the fourth, third and second spectators are on the top of the pack in that order. False shuffle and leave one indifferent card on top of the pairs.

If you have sufficient confidence, the seven top cards may be palmed off and the deck handed to a spectator to be shuffled, but this is not absolutely necessary for the repeated shuffles already made should have convinced the audience that the cards are really lost in the pack.

Show the pack face outwards in the left hand, call attention to the face card and ask if it was drawn by anyone. The answer being "No", take the pack in the right hand, showing it and repeat the question. Receiving the same reply, push the card back on the top of the deck, separate the card next to it with the left fingers and make the Herrmann pass, (page 34) with the two cards as you turn the pack face down.

Lay the cards face down on the palm of your outstretched left hand and announce that, by merely shaking the cards a little, the two cards selected by the last spectator will at once pass one to the top and the other to the bottom of the deck. Give the cards a little shake, invite the fourth spectator to name his cards and with the right hand hold up the pack with the bottom card, one of his pair, facing the audience. Replace the pack in the left hand and with the right hand lift off the top card, raise the hand and show the face of this card, the second card of the fourth pair.

As you take off this card let the left hand with the pack fall to your side as you make a slight turn to the left. The pack goes out of sight for a moment and, in that moment, rest the backs of the cards flat against the thigh, push the top card off downwards with the left thumb, press the tips of the second and third fingers on its face and draw it upwards onto the face of the deck. (Fig. I.) The two cards selected by the third spectator are thus brought to the top and bottom of the deck.

The action takes but an instant and in the meantime all attention has been concentrated on the card in your right hand. Raise the left hand to its former position and push the card in the right hand into the middle of the pack. Again give the pack a little shake and order the cards of the third spectator to pass to the top and bottom. Show these cards and, by the same maneuver pass the top card to the bottom against your left thigh, so bringing the two cards of the second spectator to the top and bottom.

Fig. i   Fig. ii   Fig. iii

Place the card just shown in the right hand into the middle of the deck and once more give it a little shake on your left hand. Reveal the cards belonging to the second spectator and remark, "Well, that disposes of all the cards chosen." Hand the deck to a spectator to be shuffled and stand at ease, both hands in trouser pockets.

The first person is sure to remind you that his pair has not been found. Pretending embarrassment, apologise for your oversight and explain that the cards having left your hands it will be quite impossible for you to find them as you did the others. "However", you say, as if recovering confidence, "perhaps I may be able to find them by a different method." In the meantime you have palmed the cards in your pocket in your right hand.

Invite the spectator, who has been shuffling the deck, to put it face down on the palm of your left hand and make a free cut. Lift the remaining cards with your right hand, adding the palmed cards, take the cut portion and put it below those in right hand, thus completing a regular cut and bringing the two cards, the first pair chosen, to the top without arousing the least suspicion. Explaining what you are about to do, secretly pass the top card to the bottom, grip the pack firmly between the thumb and fingers of the right hand, thumb on the face of the bottom card, and jerk the hand sharply upwards. Let all the cards, except the top card and the bottom card, fly up in a solid bunch about a foot into the air, close the thumb and fingers, bringing the two cards tightly together and dash the hand against the deck.

This will cause the cards to scatter in all directions, leaving the cards of the first pair between the thumb and fingers. Hold them with their backs towards the spectators, slide the cards apart, slip the second and third fingers between them and spread the fingers with the result one card is held by the thumb and first finger and the other between the second and third fingers. (Fig. III. page 22).

Invite the first spectator to name his cards and with an air of triumph turn the faces of the cards to the audience showing that you have succeeded.

This trick makes a very effective finish to a series of card tricks. The idea of having the pairs of cards of the same values is simply to make it easier for the spectator to remember them. It may seem absurd but it is a fact that when cards of different values and suits are taken, one or other of cards is often forgotten by a spectator to the great detriment of the feat.

THE "CONUS" ACES

EFFECT— The four Aces are caused to travel to different parts of the pack, they are transformed into four other cards while held by a spectator, finally they vanish and are found in one of the spectator's pockets.

REQUIREMENTS— Four duplicate Aces. One Ace, the Ace of Clubs for instance, is taken from the deck that is to be used and placed on top of the four duplicate Aces. This packet of five Aces is then crimped at the inner end and put on top of the pack.

WORKING— Invite a spectator to come up to assist and seat him behind a small table. Take up your position on his right. Show the pack, spreading the cards with the faces towards the audience, square them up and, as you turn to hand the deck to the spectator, palm the five Aces from the top with the right hand.

Give the pack to your helper, asking him to take out the Aces and at the same time satisfy himself that there are only four in the deck. As he finds the three and puts them on the table, pick them up and put them in your right hand, naming each one. He fails to find the Ace of Clubs. Turn to the audience and say "Did you see that? He's playing tricks with me already." Put the three Aces in your left hand, take the right lapel of the helper's coat, pull the coat open and thrust your right hand into his breast pocket. Bring out the top Ace of the five, Ace of Clubs, leaving the four duplicates behind.

The action must be done naturally, as if you were merely taking out a card already there and not as if you were putting something in his pocket. As the hand goes to the pocket the forefinger should be extended, pointing to it.

As you lean over to take the card, whisper to your victim, "Button up your coat just to make them laugh." He does this and it always causes amusement besides diverting attention from the fact that your hand has been placed into the pocket.

2. Hand the four Aces to the helper, cut the deck about the middle and invite him to place the four cards on top of the lower part. Drop the cut on top and square the deck. Pretend to notice that the helper is suspicious and say, "You don't believe the Aces are really in the middle? I'll show them to you." Spread the faces of the cards towards him and the audience and show the Aces together, at the same time slipping the tip of left little finger above the first two. Close the spread and, in turning the deck over, execute the Herrmann pass, (page 33) bringing two Aces to the top and two to the bottom. Lay the pack on the table.

Continue, "Now, without my touching the cards in any way, the four Aces which you have placed in the middle of the pack shall go and put themselves in such positions as you yourself shall choose. Would you like them all at the top or all at the bottom; or would you rather have them three at the top and one at the bottom; or three at the bottom and one at the top; or, say, two at the top and and two at the bottom? Kindly place your hand on the cards."

Speak rather rapidly until you reach the last choice which you accentuate slightly. This position is then almost always the one that is chosen. "Two above and two below? Very well. I simply say Passe! Take the Aces yourself."

On the rare occasions when another choice is made, take the deck in your own hands, asking "Did you feel them go? No? Well they have obeyed your wishes." In the meantime you have passed the card or cards necessary from the top to the bottom, or vice versa, and then show them, placing them on the table.

3. Take the Aces, put them on the top of the deck, and looking at your hands furtively, make a little quick motion with them, then deal the Aces face down on the table, inviting the helper to put his hand on them. "Now, sir," you continue, "you are quite sure you have the four Aces?"

The spectator, not having seen the faces of cards since they were placed on the pack and having noticed the furtive movement of your hands, naturally expresses some doubt about the matter.

"What, you are not certain? Why surely they are under your hand. I see what it is. The fact is you distrust me and perhaps you are right for those cards will change presently under your very hands and you won't know anything about it, I hope."

4. Take the Aces and show them, replace them on the top of the pack, immediately making a very palpable cut looking at your hands and as if trying to do it secretly. Then, looking the victim in the eye, make a quick remark and execute the pass bringing the Aces back to the top. "Here are the Aces," you say, dealing them off again. "Now put your hand on them."

Again the spectator is sceptical and after you expostulate with him for suspecting you of trickery, turn them face up. In the meantime you have slipped the tip of your left little finger under the top card. Place the Aces once more on top of the pack and, a moment later, take them off together with the top card of the pack. Hold them squared together so that this indifferent card is the only one visible as you show the packet to the spectator and the audience, and say, "Take notice that there has been no change. Here are the Aces." Replace the five cards on the top and deal the four Aces face down on the table.

"Put your hand on them. Now you are satisfied you have the Aces, aren't you?" The answer generally is a decisive "No." Appeal to the audience, asking if they are sure the Aces are on the table. A chorus of "Noes" the response. Expostulating, declare that you just showed them the Aces. "No, no, we saw the . . . . of . . . . " is the cry.

Don't allow your victim to turn the cards over at once, but keep up the argument for a few moments affecting reluctance to have the cards shown. Finally tell him to show the Aces to everyone. He turns them up and finds the four Aces.

5. In the meantime you have secretly turned the top five cards face upwards" keeping the tip of the left little finger under them and holding the pack upright so that these cards cannot be seen, "Really", you say, "I cannot understand why you are so skeptical. Let me convince you." Take one Ace and put it face up on top of the pack, thus covering the reversed cards, then hold the pack so everyone can see that the three other Aces go fairly on top face up.

"Now, where are the Aces?" The helper replies, "On the top." Turn the nine face up cards over, thus bringing the five indifferent cards above the Aces. "Satisfied at last," you say, "Please watch me very closely." Slowly and daintily deal off the four top cards. Show the next card, saying, "You see they have all been dealt. Put your hand on them and the other hand on that. Now I want you to give me your word that you won't move your hands from those Aces until my trick is finished. If you did the audience might think that you performed the trick and not I." This is necessary to prevent any possibility of the helper taking an untimely peek at the cards. Turn the deck face up and palm at least five cards in the left hand, immediately spreading the rest face up on the table to prove there are no Aces left in the deck.

6. Pick up the pack, add the cards palmed in the left hand and turn the pack face downwards. There is one indifferent card on the top, the four Aces following it. False shuffle, jogging one card and shuffling off. Cut at the jog to bring the cards back to the same position. Take off the indifferent card, show it and continue, "Now for the four Aces. I won't bring them here into my hand but here on the table, the effect will be more surprising." At the words "into my hand" make a careless gesture towards the pack and top change the card for the first Ace. Put it face down on the table.

False shuffle, getting rid of the top card and bringing the three Aces back to the top. Double lift, taking the two top Aces, hold them out to your victim as one card and ask him to breathe on it. "Oh", you exclaim, "I didn't ask you to blow on the card. You've made two." Spread the cards apart and place them down with the first Ace.

7. Ask your helper to release one hand, take a card from the deck and show it to everybody. Palm the last Ace in the right hand, take the selected card in your left hand and put the pack on the table.

Shift the card to your right hand, adding the palmed card to it and hold them squared as one card. "Now", you continue, "would you like me to change this last card into an Ace visibly or invisibly?" The answer is always "Visibly."

"Visibly? Nothing could be simpler. Watch. I simply pass my hand over the card three times and it changes into an Ace."

To do this, take the card between the left thumb and fingers, thumb on the face, fingers at the back, Fig. I, turn to the left and hold the card(s) facing the audience. Show the right hand and pass it over the face of the card, counting "One." Repeat the movement, but this time push the rear card, the Ace, into the right hand and change the left hand grip of the visible card by shifting the fingers to the opposite side, Fig. II, counting "Two." Once more pass the right hand over the card, counting "Three" and leaving the Ace on the face of the card in the left hand. The left thumb and fingers keep the cards squared.

FIG. I

FIG. II

"One Ace," you say triumphantly. Pick up one of the three on the table, add it in front of the first in the left hand, "Two Aces," and do the same with the remaining two. "All four Aces. Turn up your four cards and see what I have sent you." He turns up his cards and finds four indifferent ones.

In the general amusement caused by the victim's discomfiture slip the indifferent card from the back of the Aces on to the pack which you have taken in your left hand and throw the four Aces on the table face up.

8. While you are congratulating your helper on the ability he has shown and assuring him that with a little more practice he should develop into a very fair magician, casually pick up the Aces, place them on the top and immediately palm them off, then hold the pack in the same hand. "I will prove," you continue, "to you that you are really a better magician than you think. Take the whole pack and hold it above your head, so." Place the pack in his hand and raise it above his head. "You have simply to order the Aces to leave the pack and pass into one of your pockets and they will do so. Just say Passe!"

He does this, then runs through the deck and finds that the Aces are missing. He searches his pockets and finally finds the four Aces in his inside coat pocket. In the meantime you have placed both hands casually in your trousers pockets and so disposed of the palmed Aces. The duplicate Aces were inserted in the spectator's pocket so long before that the fact that you even touched him is quite lost sight of.

This routine is most effective for club or platform work, much more so than the usual Ace routine in which packets of four cards with an Ace at the bottom of each are made, and it is hard to understand why the masterpiece of the oldtime magician, Conus, or some modification of it, as above, has been so neglected. It is a "talky" trick and calls for good management of the voluntary assistant but constant movement gives ample cover for all the necessary moves.

PART II.

NEW COLOR CHANGES

Ever since the invention of the first Color Change by Mons. Trewey, the celebrated French Fantaisist and Magician, all the various modifications of the original trick have been done by means of the regular palm, that is to say, the stolen card lies along the length of the hand. It is quite possible to produce the effect with the card to be produced lying across the fingers. The effect is thus enhanced since the width of the fingers is evidently insufficient to conceal a card. I will explain two methods for producing the effect.

I. THE VISIBLE COLOR CHANGE

EFFECT— The face card of the deck suddenly and visibly changes without being covered by the right hand.

METHOD— Hold the deck upright in the left hand, the thumb on the middle of one side, second and third fingers on the other, the forefinger on the upper end and the little finger free, the bottom card facing the spectators, Fig. 1.

Bring the right hand over to the left hand and take the lower end of the deck between the thumb and forefinger, push the rear card downwards with the left forefinger and with the right thumb push the lower end of this card between the right first and second fingers which nip it tightly without allowing any part of the card to protrude to the front. Fig. 2.

Let the upper end of this card drop by lifting the right thumb out of the way momentarily, so that it is at right angles to the deck, and at once grip the bottom end of the deck with the right thumb and forefinger. Fig. 3. Remove the left hand and with a careless gesture show it empty.

Bring the left hand back to the deck and take it by the lower corners between the left thumb and forefinger, at the same moment press the heel of that hand on the free end of the stolen card, bending the card downwards until this outer end is gripped between the right third and little fingers. Do not allow any part of the card to protrude to the front. Move the left hand away, the right hand remaining stationary for a moment or two. The stolen card is now held lengthwise across the fingers of the right hand, the upper index corner between the tips of the first and second fingers and the opposite lower corner between the third and fourth finger tips. Fig. 4.

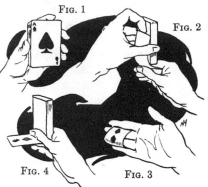

Pass the right hand downwards over the face of the deck several times, at the third passage, when the right forefinger is opposite and a little in front of the bottom of the deck, bend the right thumb under the clipped card and push it upwards, at the same moment releasing its lower end from the third and fourth fingers. The card at once flies up, face outwards, covering the face card of the deck against which it is held by the left thumb and fingers, the right hand moving away. The change is instantaneous.

II. THE ROLL DOWN COLOR CHANGE

Hold the deck and steal the rear card in exactly the same way as in No. 1. Bring the right hand in front of the deck letting the free end of the stolen card touch the top of the face card just under the tip of the left forefinger. Fig. 1.

Keeping the fingers of the right hand pressed closely together, bring the hand towards the deck and bend the stolen card almost in half, allowing the lower half of the face card to be visible from the front. Fig. 2.

Move the right hand slowly downwards over the face of the deck bringing the stolen card into view from the top downwards and leaving it on the face of the deck.

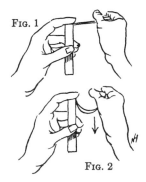

Note. After this manuscript was in the hands of the printers I found that Mr. Cul-pitt in the Magic Wand for June-Sept. p. 76. has described a color change using the same principle of the stolen card projecting at right angles from the fingers. In his method, however, the steal is made from the upper end of the deck and the change is made by rolling the card upwards. Apparently we have both been using the same principle independently for a number of years.

III. COLOR CHANGE WITH FINGERS WIDE APART

Stand with your right side to the front, hold the deck in the left hand in the usual position for making the color change, that is on its side face outwards and vertical, the thumb on the upper side, the fore-finger at the middle of the outer end and the other three fingers on the lower side.

Pass the right hand with the fingers spread wide apart over the face card with a circular motion outward and downward, the roots of the fingers passing just beyond the outer end of the pack. Then show the right hand empty.

Repeat the circular movement and at the moment when the palm of the right hand covers the face card and the fingers protrude beyond it, push the rear card of the deck forward with the left forefinger and clip its outer end between the roots of the right first and little fingers, carry-ing it away. There must be no stoppage of the circular movement which continues on its way over the face card, downwards, backwards, up-wards and again over the face card, this time depositing the stolen card squarely on the bottom card. At once draw the hand back over the face card with the fingers spread wide apart.

The inner, free end of the clipped card will project an inch or more above the palm itself but if the hand is kept with its back squarely to the front there is no danger of the card being exposed.

PART III.

THE RIFFLE PASS. I.

This pass was, I believe, originated by the late Dr. Wm. Elliott. It was explained to me a good many years ago and while I never had an opportunity of seeing it done by Dr. Elliott I am told that the method given below was one used by him. The riffle pass is now known to many performers and it seems to me that the time has come to give credit to the inventor.

The preliminary moves are exactly the same as for the classical pass. That is, the tip of the little finger is inserted between the two packets. The upper packet is gripped between the little finger and the other three fingers of the left hand, while the lower packet is held by the right thumb at the inner end and the top joint of the right second finger at the outer end, the packet being pressed firmly into the fork of the left thumb.

The upper packet is drawn off by the left fingers and the lower one raised bookwise by the right thumb and second finger. As soon as the packets clear one another, the left fingers are closed bringing their packet under that in the right hand the cards of which are immediately riffled down on top by the right second finger, the left thumb pressing down firmly on the middle of the back of the packet.

Neatly done the action forms an optical illusion. The left hand packet appears to fall as the first cards of the riffle. It helps greatly to have the pack divided rather nearer the top than the middle so that the original lower packet will contain more cards than the upper one. In this way more cards are really riffled and the illusion is greater.

The first part of the action should be made with a slight downward move of the hands under cover of the back of the right hand, then the riffle is made with an upward movement of the hands. A riffle of the whole pack should follow at once accompanied by the same movements of the hands, down and up.

THE RIFFLE PASS. II.
P. W. MILLER

I am indebted to Mr. P. W. Miller, of Susanville, California, for this version of the riffle pass.

A card having been selected, returned and a break above it having been secured with the tip of the left little finger, proceed as follows:

1. After a few moments delay, bring the right hand over the pack, the thumb at the inner end, first finger tip on the middle of the top card, second and third fingers at the outer end, little finger on the top outer corner.

2. Slide the top packet above the break a little to the right on to the left second, third and little fingers.

3. Turn slightly to the left and with a little up and down movement of the hands riffle the cards of the upper packet with the right fingers.

4. At the same time drop the left thumb on the outer left top corner of the lower packet, bend the left first finger under this packet and raise it bookwise, hinged in the left thumb fork.

5. Complete the riffling of the upper packet and close the other packet down on top.

6. With the same slight up and down motion of the hands riffle the whole deck once or twice.

RIGHT HAND—
NOT SHOWN—
RIFFLES THIS
PACKET

This pass is fast, easy of execution and imperceptible, being covered by the back of the right hand. The riffling of the whole deck after the completion of the pass is merely for misdirection.

THE HERRMANN PASS

Probably more effort has been expended by magicians in attempting to devise an invisible pass than on any other sleight in the whole range of card conjuring. Yet an imperceptible pass has been in existence for many years and completely overlooked by the majority of magicians. The pass I refer to is the Herrmann pass, but whether it was originated by either Carl or Alexander Herrmann is not known, although it is on record that the sleight was a favorite with Alexander Herrmann.

The only reason for this neglect is the fact that the sleight has not been clearly explained, the one vital movement being omitted. This misconception in regard to its execution is so marked that a recent French author, M. Remi Ceillier, after minutely describing many other passes, dismisses the Herrmann pass as a mere curiosity. The fact remains that if this sleight is executed with the proper misdirection it is invisible no matter how closely one may watch.

The moves are very easy and with a clear understanding of the misdirection employed it can be mastered in a tithe of the time required for the regular pass. The five moves detailed below should be followed with the deck in the hands and it will be found that they blend smoothly into the simple action of turning the deck face up.

1. Hold the deck by its sides in the left hand between the thumb on one side and the second and third fingers on the other. Fig. I. bend the first and fourth fingers inwards, the nails touching the face of the bottom card.

2. Bring the right hand over the deck and grip the upper half by the ends between the thumb at the inner end and the first two fingers near the right corner of the outer end. Fig. 2.

3. Under cover of the right hand pull the lower half of the deck downwards sufficiently to allow for the insertion of the top joints of the second and third fingers of the left hand, Fig. 3, and grip this lower packet firmly between these two fingers above it and the top joints of the first and fourth fingers already bent under it.

4. Turn the deck to a vertical position with its back directly towards the spectators and by straightening the left fingers tilt the lower packet downwards, its outer end sliding down the face of the bottom card of the upper packet, until it reaches the position shown in Fig. 4.

5. At that moment the right hand, aided by an outward pressure of the tip of the left thumb on the middle of the upper side, tilts its packet to the right with exactly the same action as if the whole pack were turned over; at the same time the left fingers tilt the outer sides of its packet upwards, the edges of the two packets just clearing one another and sliding together smoothly as the left thumb draws back over the face card of the right hand packet, which now becomes the face card of the whole deck. The tips of the left second and third fingers press upwards against the back of the lower packet, aiding the turn, and are then extended to grip the outer side of the deck, which is then held between them and the left thumb, on the upper side, as in Fig. I., the pack now facing outwards.

In the action the hands are raised a little and a slight turn to the left is made. Finally the right hand lightly squares the cards as attention is called to the bottom card.

Once the principle of the sleight has been fully understood and the simple moves mastered the number of uses it can be put to, apart from simply bringing a card to the top, will be found quite surprising. For

example in the trick of the Conus Aces, page 23, when you show that
the Aces really are in the middle, for which purpose you hold the cards
facing the spectators, it is only necessary to slip the tips of the two
middle fingers of the left hand between them and make the Herrmann
pass in turning the deck face down again.

No great speed is required in the action, just a smooth imitation of
the act of turning the whole deck over when in reality only the upper
half is so turned, the movement of the lower half being completely
hidden by the back of the right hand.

I am indebted to Mr. P. W. Miller, noted card expert, who has used
this pass for many years, for the following description of the whole
action. Hold the deck a little below the waist line for the replacement
of the chosen card, then turn slowly to the left, raising the hands about
midway to shoulder height as the pass is made. The back of the right
hand then affords perfect cover and there is no movement of the fingers
to be seen.

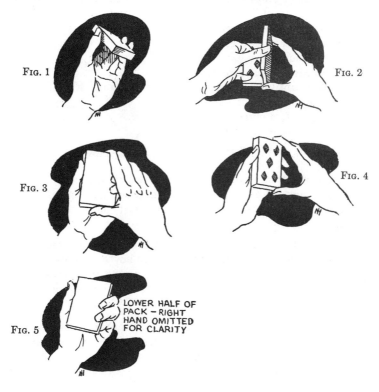

FIG. 1

FIG. 2

FIG. 3

FIG. 4

FIG. 5   LOWER HALF OF
PACK — RIGHT
HAND OMITTED
FOR CLARITY

THE "SPRING" FORCE

This easy and effective method of forcing cards is, I believe, of French origin and does not appear to be well known on this side.

1. Hold the left hand, palm upwards, at about waist height and spring the cards face up into it from above with the right hand. Stop about halfway in the flourish and call attention to the card on the top of those in the left hand, then complete the springing.

2. Repeat the action, showing another card and point out that it would be quite impossible for you to stop the springing at the same card twice, or indeed, at any particular card. Do this several times to convince the onlookers that any card stopped at must be arrived at by pure chance.

3. Turn your head away and invite a spectator to note the card you will stop at. This time spring all the cards but one, the last card of the deck, which you retain in the right hand. Hold this hand with its back to the spectators and let the cards in the left hand slant downwards against the top joints of the first and second fingers, so making it impossible for the spectator to see how many cards have been sprung. (See Fig.) Even if anyone looks at your right hand he cannot tell how many cards you have retained since the face of the single card is vertical and there might be any number of cards behind it. As a matter of fact everyone looks at the face card of those in the left hand and this is the card your victim notes.

4. Slap the right hand with its card down on the cards in the left hand, covering the noted card, thus bringing it second from the face of the deck, though to the eyes of the spectators it has been buried in the pack.

5. Turn the deck face downwards and make an overhand shuffle by pulling out all the cards but the top and bottom cards and then shuffling off, finishing by placing the last card, the card forced, on the top of the deck. The card is then dealt with as may be necessary for the trick in hand.

As many cards as you wish can be forced in exactly the same way and, if preferred, instead of shuffling the cards to the top, as explained above, the side slip can be used. It is merely necessary to turn the deck face downwards, thumb off the inner end of the bottom card, insert the tips of the left second and third fingers above it and press the next (chosen) card out into the right hand in the regular side slip sleight, and leave it on the top of the pack.

It must be remembered that the cards will lie on the top of the deck in the reverse order to that in which they were selected. The French magician, Frackson, makes very clever use of this sleight by forcing as many as seven or eight cards in succession and revealing them in different ways.

NEW LIGHT ON THE GLIDE

It is passing strange that this sleight, so old (it was explained by M. Ponsin in his book, the first technical treatise on conjuring, "Nouvelle Magie Blanche Devoilee", published in 1853) and still so much used, has never been properly described. In all the textbooks two very important details are omitted.

THE CORRECT METHOD IS THIS:

1. Hold the deck face down by its sides in the left hand between the thumb and the first, second and third fingers, the little finger being free and the thumb a little below the middle of the side. Fig. 1.

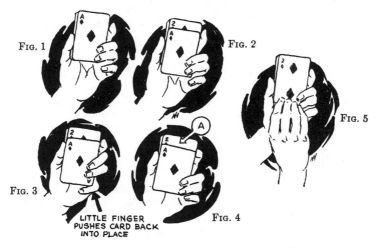

Fig. 1

Fig. 2

Fig. 5

Fig. 3

LITTLE FINGER
PUSHES CARD BACK
INTO PLACE

Fig. 4

2. Raise the deck to show the bottom card to the spectators; then turn it down and, with the tips of the second and third fingers, slide the bottom card half an inch or a little more towards the wrist. Fig. 2. With the tip of the right second finger draw out the next card by its outer end, thus apparently taking off the card just shown.

3. In this form the sleight is an easy way of making a change. It is, however, more often used to produce a chosen card at a given number. To do this the card is brought second from the bottom by means of a shuffle. A number having been called, the bottom card is shown, the pack turned face down and this card is drawn off and dealt face up, proving all fair. The next card, the one chosen, is slid back by means of the glide and the card above it drawn out as being the second card, This process is continued until the number is reached and it is at this point that the sleight is imperfectly executed. All the other cards have been pulled out from the very end of the deck, but to reach and produce the card that has been slid back, the fingers have to be pushed right under the pack to secure it. This is wrong and is quite noticeable to an observant person.

4. The correct method is to push the card flush with the rest by means of the second joint of the left little finger. The action is completely under cover and the card can then be taken away with the tip of the second finger in exactly the same way as the preceding cards. Fig. 3.

The second point in which the explanations of the glide are defective is this: After having made the move and drawn out the next card it is very often necessary to turn the pack upwards to show that another card is on the bottom. In order to do this the textbooks say to draw off the card which has been slid back, put it on the top the pack, without showing its face, and then hold up the pack showing a new card on the bottom. There is absolutely no reason for taking a card from the bottom and putting it on the top and therefore the move arouses suspicion.

The correct method is this: After having drawn out the second card, grip the outer end of the deck with the right thumb on top, Fig. 4. A., the fingers on the face of the pack, and draw it outwards until it almost clears the card that was drawn back, which is retained in the left hand, turn the deck over lengthwise, bringing it face up and at the same moment turn the left hand palm upwards. The pack is thus brought face up on top of the original bottom card which then becomes the top card of the deck.

Smoothly done with a slight natural swing of the hands upwards the transference of the card from the bottom to the top of the deck is imperceptible and the appearance of a new card on the bottom is, to the layman, proof positive that the card first chosen has in fact been dealt on the table.

NEW FINGER CLIP PALM

The word "palm" in magical parlance has acquired the meaning of holding an object secretly in the hand whether it is held in the palm itself or with the fingers and it appears to be useless to try to restrict it to actual palming. The movement to be described is really a finger clip or hold only, the palm of the hand takes no part in it.

Hold the deck in the usual position for squaring it in the left hand, the second joint of the thumb on one side, the second joints of the second, third and fourth fingers on the other side and the forefinger bent under the deck resting against the bottom card. Fig. 1.

Turn to the left and bring the right hand over the pack, the thumb on the inner end and the tips of the four fingers, held close together on the outer end. After squaring the sides and the ends of the deck, separate some half a dozen cards with the right thumb at the top of the inner end and push them forward about half an inch. Fig. 2.

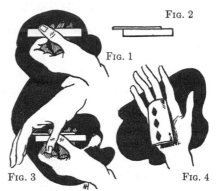

Fig. 2

Fig. 1

Fig. 3

Fig. 4

Push the right hand forward, bending the fingers at right angles to the back of the hand and clip the projecting end of the packet between the roots of the first and fourth fingers. Fig. 3.

At once drop the thumb on the back of the pack at the inner end and grip it against the tips of the first three fingers. Remove the left hand and show it with a careless wave.

Take the pack with the left hand, the right hand remaining stationary for a moment then dropping naturally. The clipped cards will project from it almost at a right angle. Fig. 4.

PRODUCTION OF THE CARDS IN A FAN FROM THE FINGER CLIP PALM

Having secured a packet of cards in the right as explained and still facing left, stretch out the left hand with the pack and execute a one hand flourish, the continuous Charlier pass, for example. The right hand remains still, the fingers slightly spread and the forefinger pointing to the left hand.

At the end of the left hand maneuver, thrust out the right hand to the left letting the clipped cards swing forward against the fingers, drop the point of the thumb to the inner end of the packet and rapidly spread the cards in a wide fan. The thumb spreads them to the right and the first and second fingers by closing in on the palm spread them towards the left, the result being a perfect, wide fan of c a r d s produced apparently from the air.

NEW THROW CHANGE OF A PACKET OF CARDS

In Card Manipulations No. II. a method of changing several cards by means of the Hand to Hand Palm Change has been described. Here is another method in which one hand only is used. Let us suppose by way of example that at the end of a trick with the four Aces you wish to get possession of them, yet apparently leave them in view.

1. Palm four cards in the right hand and to avoid bending them hold the pack in the same hand.

2. Pick up the four Aces with the left hand and show t h e m, put the pack down on the table towards the left and take the A c e s in the right h a n d as in Fig. 1.

3. Close this little fan of cards with the left hand from right to left and leave the four cards held by their ends between the right thumb at the inner ends and the fingers at the outer ends, the forefinger at one corner and the little finger at the other. Fig. 2.

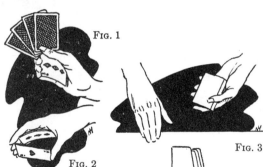

Fig. 1

Fig. 2

Fig. 3

4. Take the pack in the left hand and make a motion of placing the Aces on the top, but stop and with a slight throwing motion from right to left, release the palmed cards, so that they fall flat on the table and palm the Aces in their place.

5. Continue the motion of the right hand towards the left, take the pack in that hand, adding the palmed Aces to the top in the action.

In order to avoid bending the palmed cards they should be held by the pressure of the little finger tip on the outer right corner and the base of the thumb on the inner left corner. The sleight should not be done with more than eight or ten cards at most.

Mr. Fred Braue points out that this change can be mabe even more effectively by apparently throwing the cards into the left hand really making the change. The left hand is then raised showing the cards, backs outwards, and the right hand casually picks up the deck adding the palmed cards to it.

REPLACING A PALMED CARD ON THE TOP OF THE DECK

In "Card Manipulations No. IV., p. 87. et seq." I have treated this sleight almost exhaustively but the fact remains that the placing of the hand with the palmed card flat on the deck, even if for a moment only, is not natural. To take the pack naturally, either from the hands of a spectator or from your left hand, it is grasped by the fingers at the outer end and the thumb at the inner end, the rest of the hand being arched over the cards, and the problem is to replace the palmed card on the top without bringing the hand down flat. I am indebted to Mr. Frederick Braue, of Alameda, California, a valued correspondent, for the solution which is a very simple one and, once known, appears perfectly obvious, but it is just these simple actions which require a touch of genius to discover.

This ideal procedure is simply the working of the top one hand palm, "Card Manipulations No. I. p. 2.," exactly in reverse. We will suppose that you have a card palmed in the right hand and a spectator has shuffled the pack. Take it from him with your right hand, the tips of the fingers at the outer end and the thumb at the inner end. Bend the little finger inward and press it on the back of the palmed card, pushing it down on to the top of the pack as you place the pack in the left hand and immediately square the pack in the usual way. The right hand remains arched over the pack throughout, the palm not coming in contact with it for a moment.

The action is exactly the same when a packet of cards has to be replaced on the top, but in this case the little finger must be pressed firmly on the back of the packet until the cards are actually put in the left hand, to prevent any of the cards slipping out.

To some performers, indeed, I am afraid to many, this insistence upon perfection in detail may seem unnecessary, but this is only because so many magicians do not give their audiences credit for ordinary intelligence. I ask my readers who have never considered this subject carefully to watch the action next time they see a performer replace palmed cards on the deck and then ask themselves if the fact that an addition of something to the top of the deck has not been plainly indicated. The correct method, as discovered by Mr. Braue, is so simple and easy that there is no excuse for it not being adopted.

This same difficulty has been recognized by French magicians and it is interesting to note the solution they have arrived at. I quote from M. Remi Ceillier's book, "Manuel pratique d'Illusionisme et de Prestidigitation"——

"As the pack is much shorter than the hand this has to be arched to touch the ends and there is no natural reason to spread it flat on the pack. So it is necessary to take the pack in the left hand (supposing that it is the right hand which holds the card palmed) and put it in the right hand which is turned upwards to receive it. The public should be a little to your right."

It seems to me that there are two fatal objections to this method, first, the unnatural taking of the pack with the left hand, and, second, the laying of the deck face upwards on the right hand.

THE TOP AND BOTTOM CHANGES

"I know of nothing more surprising than the effect of a card neatly changed", so says Robert-Houdin in his book "Les Secrets de la Prestidigitation et de Magie." But if the great master could see the efforts of modern card conjurers he would probably alter his saying to, "I know of nothing more surprising than the clumsy execution of the top change."

In a long period devoted to magic I have met many magicians, professionals and amateurs, and I can recall one only who made the top change correctly, that is, invisibly. Before going into the reasons for this curious fact, let me define the terms 'top change' and 'bottom change', for there is confusion amongst card men even here. The top change is that in which the card to be changed is left on the TOP of the deck, and the bottom change is that in which the card to be changed is left on the bottom of the deck. In both cases the substitute card is taken from the top of the pack.

Both these changes are clumsily done by modern conjurers because modern textbooks give, in the case of the top change, an entirely wrong method of fingering, and, in both cases, incomplete explanations. I will deal with the top change first.

I. THE TOP CHANGE

Ponsin in 1853, Robert-Houdin in 1868 and Hoffmann in 1874, all give the correct method but, somewhere in the latter part of the last century, a so-called easier method of fingering was introduced and in 1902 Roterberg in "New Era Card Tricks" and Erdnase in "The Expert At The Card Table" gave this as being the correct way to make the top change. They were followed in this by Hatton and Plate in "Magicians' Tricks" and since that time this modern method has been the only one referred to in later writings. The result has been that this beautiful move, the invisible top change, has been lost to magicians for it is impossible to achieve it with the method thus set forth.

In his instructions Roterberg says, "the top card of the pack is quickly seized by the *first* and *second* fingers of the right hand which is immediately *withdrawn*." (Italics mine). Two statements and both wrong. It must be perfectly plain that if these instructions are carried out an attentive observer would see, first, a card held between the performer's thumb and fingers, a snatch from the pack and then a card held between the performer's first and second fingers. One might practice till Doomsday and not achieve an invisible change from these directions. It is no wonder that the top change is done so badly by the present generation of card conjurers.

Close attention to the following explanation and a modicum of practice will enable the student to make a top change that is imperceptible, no matter how closely a spectator watches the card and the performer's hands.

THE CORRECT METHOD:

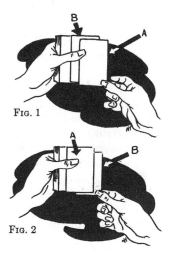

Fig. 1

Fig. 2

1. With the right hand take the card A. which is to be changed, by its lower right hand corner between the ball of the thumb and the second joint of the middle finger, the first finger being held free alongside the second finger.

2. The card B., for which A. is to be exchanged, lies on the top of the pack. With the left thumb push this card, B., over the side of the deck to the right about an inch.

3. Bring the right hand over to the left hand, release A. on the top of the pack, the left thumb being raised slightly to allow for its passage, and seize the protruding corner of B. with the tips of the right thumb and forefinger. Fig. 1.

4. At the same moment drop the left thumb on the back of A., draw it flush with the rest of the deck and move the left hand away, the right hand remaining stationary or moving slightly to the left following

the left hand, thus separating the hands to the same extent as at the start of the movement. On no account must the right hand be drawn back to the right. Fig. 2.

The hands must not be held close to the body, they should be extended freely, the elbows only being near the body, and the left thumb must push out the top card of the deck just an instant before the right thumb and forefinger are ready to seize it. Two common faults are, the holding of the hands quite close to the body, giving the impression some movement is being concealed, and the pushing out of the top card before the hands start their swing. It will be noted that by holding the right hand card at the extreme right lower corner the hands are further apart throughout the move and this helps to complete the illusion that they do not come together at all.

When the action is thoroughly understood, practice the sleight while saying, "I will put the card on the table so"; stand with the table on your left, with the hands about a foot apart and at the same height and, as you swing around to the left, move the right hand a little faster than the left, the hands coming together in the middle of the turn, make the change, then move the left hand away a little faster than the right so that when the right hand arrives over the table the left hand is again about a foot away from it. There must be no stoppage in the swing to the left and no snatching of the card. As the right hand receives the card it follows through with the result that, neatly executed, the turn of the whole body to the left completely covers the smaller movement of the hands and to the eyes of the spectator they do not come together at all.

Great speed is not necessary, just make the turn naturally and remember that it is the movement of the left hand away from the right that wholly disguises the operation.

Again, you may say, "You see I do not use the pack for a moment. Will you hold the card?" at the same time making an indicatory gesture with the right hand towards the pack, executing the change and moving the left hand with the pack away.

I know of no sleight in the whole range of card conjuring that gives the operator so great a 'kick' as the imperceptible change of a card right under the noses of the onlookers while they are being asked to see that no such change takes place. I trust that this explanation of the top change will be the means of resurrecting this most potent weapon of the old masters.

II. THE BOTTOM CHANGE

This change is an easier one but not nearly so perfect although the illusion has the same basis, the swing of the body and the withdrawal of the left hand from the right after the exchange has been made. It has, however, one great advantage over the top change, it can be done with equal facility with any number of cards.

METHOD— 1. Hold the card A. in the right hand between the thumb and the first two fingers in the same way as for the top change except that it is held at the middle of the right hand side instead of by the lower corner.

2. Hold the pack in the left hand in front of the body and about a foot away from the right hand. Push the top card, B., over the side of the pack to the right about an inch.

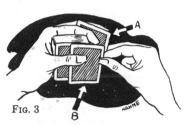

Fig. 3

The pack must be held well down in the fork of the left hand by pressing the top two joints of the first finger on the side of the pack just below the top right hand corner. The second, third and fourth fingers of the left hand are free.

3. Make a turn to the left and bring the right hand over to the left hand at the same time moving the forefinger from below A. on to its back so that A. is then gripped by the first two fingers leaving the thumb free.

4. As the hands come together in front of the body, the right hand having moved a little faster than the left, deposit A. under the pack, the last three fingers of the left hand opening to receive it and then closing on it to retain it, and at the same moment seize B. with the tips of the right thumb and forefinger. Fig. 3.

5. Continue the swing to the left with both hands but move the left hand away a little faster than the right so that at the end of the movement the hands are again the same distance apart. Then drop the left hand a little and with the left fingers draw the card A. perfectly flush with the rest of the deck.

The right hand completes the movement by placing the card on the table, on a chair seat, dropping it to the floor, etc., as may be necessary for the trick in hand.

Here again the illusion of the larger movement of the body covering the smaller movement of the hands comes into play, and neatly done the actual meeting of the hands in front of the body is imperceptible to the onlooker. And again, great speed is not required, the swing should be made at the natural pace that would be used if no change were being made.

As soon as the movements of the fingers and the hands have been coordinated the sleight should be practiced in the act of turning to the left place the card on a table. First actually put the card down, then repeat the turn to the left, executing the change and copying the first action as closely as possible.

When facility has been acquired the change can be made in the action of turning to the left to rub the card on the left sleeve. As before the change is actually made as the hands pass in front of the body and they should be about a foot apart when the left arm is stretched out and the card is applied to the sleeve by the right hand. The change can also be made in rubbing the card on the left thigh or in the action of placing the card on the floor.

Particular note should be made of the fact that this change can be made with a single card in each hand or with a packet of cards in each hand, both these moves being very useful. Exactly the same sleight can be executed for exchanging an envelope for the top one of a packet, one slate for another or one linking ring for another.

The two great faults to be avoided are, first, holding the card A. between the first and second fingers when showing it before the change and, second, moving the right hand away from the left after the change has been made.

LOCATIONS

It is now a good many years since I introduced the automatic jogging of a card returned to a left hand fan which is then closed by the right hand from left to right, the pack being reversed in the action. The outer end of the deck being then squared by tapping it with the right fingers, the chosen card is jogged at the inner end. By drawing back the top card a little the pack can be placed on the table while the sleeves are pulled back, for example, and the card can be found instantly when the pack is picked up.

At about the same time, Mr. Walter Gibson applied the same idea in this manner—in replacing the right hand portion of the deck after the return of the chosen card, this card was pushed slightly back with the tip of the right thumb, thus jogging it. A slight pull back of the top card, then allowed him to put the pack down as described.

I have also been told that, for a number of years, Mr. Judah has used a similar idea for delaying the pass. Quite recently Mr. Nate Leipzig, in the Sphinx, described his method of jogging a card after its return to a riffled deck which was then placed aside after drawing back the top card.

In the following article, which is, I think, one of the most valuable contributions to card manipulation of recent years, Mr. Braue has developed the idea to an almost incredible extent. By using any of the methods he explains it would seem, even to a conjurer ignorant of the ruse employed, quite impossible for the operator to keep track of the chosen card. Thus even a simple discovery becomes somewhat of a miracle.

THE DELAYED LOCATION
(Braue)

I. ON THE TABLE

Upon the return of a chosen card to the deck, jog it at the right hand side of the pack. Holding the cards between the right thumb at the inner ends and the second and third fingers on the outer ends, rest the right forefinger on the left side of the pack and bevel the cards to the right so that they lie in a short ribbon. See Illustration. The jogged position of the chosen card is thus concealed.

Pick up the pack by drawing it off the table towards the body. As it leaves the table press the left fingers upwards against the bottom card thus pressing the the pack flat against the right palm and holding the cards rigidly in position. Grasp the pack between the left thumb and fingers and then take the pack with the right hand by the ends.

With the left thumb square the pack by rubbing its left side, exerting pressure towards the right. When the pack is squared the card originally jogged will still be in that position.

II. THE SPRING

a. Onto The Table— A chosen card having been returned to the deck, jog it at the right side. A deceptive way to do this is to riffle the end of the pack and allow the card to be inserted for only three-fourths of its length. Place the right hand over the pack, resting the second and third fingers against the outer end of the protruding card and the right forefinger at the outer left corner of the pack. With the two fingers push the card flush with the pack, apparently, it goes squarely into the deck, but actually, the right forefinger automatically causes the card to be jogged at the right side, a fact which is concealed by the right fingers.

Another method is to form a break under the desired card, and insert the tip of the little finger at the inner right corner. Applying pressure upward, force the inner right corner of the chosen card to the right. Catch the outer right corner with the tip of the right little finger and press it backward. This double action jogs the card to the right.

Standing with the left side to the front, the jogged card concealed by the fingers of the right hand and the position of the pack, spring the cards upon the table. The pack should be held an inch or two above the table top at an angle of about forty-five degrees so that the cards spring flat against the table.

As you spring the cards move the hand slightly to the right, causing them to lie in a short ribbon with the left edges beveled. They are then in seeming disorder.

When later you wish to establish control over the chosen card, pick up the pack by placing the right fingers at the outer end and sweep the cards backward off the table into your left hand which presses upward against the bottom cards with the tips of the second and third fingers thus keeping the cards flat against the palm of the right hand. The cards are thus held rigidly in the same position as they were on the table.

Take the cards, still in apparent disorder, between the left fingers underneath and the thumb on top, then grasp the ends with the right hand. Square the pack by rubbing the left thumb back and forth against the left edges of the cards, exerting pressure to the right.

You will find that the pack is now perfectly squared, and that the card originally jogged at the right side remains jogged and may be shifted to the top or bottom by any sleight, since the little finger can easily curl over the card and form a break above it.

The move gains by being performed casually; indeed there is no reason why you should not be casual in the action for, despite the rough manner in which the cards are handled, it is almost impossible, even by intent, to lose the jog. Paradoxically, to your spectator it seems impossible for you to have even the faintest notion as to the location of his card.

b. Into The Hand— The principle here is practically the same as in springing the cards onto the table. The pack, with the card jogged on the right side, is held an inch or so above the left palm. The cards are sprung onto the extended left hand, the right hand moving slightly to the right in the action. The rest follows as in "a".

CARD CONTROL

I. JOG AND ONE HAND FAN

After a chosen card has been replaced in the pack, jog it at the right hand side of the deck. Take the pack by the outer end, fingers below and thumb on top, and, with the pack still parallel with the floor, execute the one hand fan.

This may be done either as a casual flourish or you may invite the spectator to note that his card actually remains in the center of the pack.

(Nevertheless, he cannot see his card, no matter how closely he may look, but you do not give him time to discover this fact. What you are doing really is to impress upon him the fact that you cannot possibly manipulate the cards. The manner in which the pack is held, peculiar to one hand fans, assures him that apparently you cannot control his card.) If cards with all-over back patterns are used, the back of the fan may be shown casually.

In this, as with all other forms of jog location, never say, "Look— Note that I do not hold a break, crimp the card, use short cards or strippers, etc." Your spectator, if he is at all intelligent—(and he is)—will note these facts without your calling attention to other subterfuges which you may have occasion to use later.

Close the fan with the right hand, at the same time bringing the outer end inward toward the body. Thus the pack is in the same position as when you first made the fan. Grasp the pack at the top and bottom with the left thumb and fingers; then transfer it to the right hand, taking it by the ends. Square the sides of the pack by rubbing the left thumb back and forth against its left side, exerting pressure towards the right. When the pack is squared, the card originally jogged will still be jogged and available for any further manipulation.

The entire move should be performed slowly and, so engrossed should you be in addressing the spectators, that not once should you glance at the pack; apparently the location of the chosen card is of not the least interest to you and your whole manner should reflect this sublime indifference.

II. FAN CONTROL

a/. In this move control is established over a card which the spectator himself inserts in a fanned deck.

Hold the pack in the right hand and fan it with the left fingers. A one-hand fan cannot be used. Extend the fan of cards in the right hand for the replacement of a chosen card. If the spectator pushes his card completely into the fan you will find that, if you hold the cards fairly loosely, the card above and the card below the chosen card will be pushed inward a quarter inch or more.

Most spectators, however, push the card in until a half inch remains protruding from beyond from the end of the fan. In such case place your left forefinger against the left outer corner of the chosen card and push it fairly into the fan. This, by friction, jogs the cards above and below, at the inner end, a quarter inch or more.

Close the fan slowly by placing the left fingers against the right end of the fan and moving the hand to the left. The inner ends of the cards pivot on the right thumb at the top and the fingers at the bottom of the pack. When the fan is closed the former outer end is nearest the body.

The left hand takes the pack at the sides, thumb at the left side, second, third and fourth fingers at the right side, the forefinger extended but not touching the outer end. This last finger squares the deck by pressing inward against the outer end. This action forces the chosen card out of the inner end of the pack, jogging the card from an eighth to a quarter of an inch. At the same moment drop the pack from the left fingers into the palm of the hand where it is held loosely, the jogged card being perfectly concealed.

You can now bring the card to the bottom or the top by the pass, shuffle or any other method you prefer.

b/. Riffle Control.

Another method of handling is to riffle the ends of the cards for the return of the chosen card. Prevent it from being pushed flush with the pack by holding the inner end tightly, explaining, if you like, that you wish to assure your spectators that the card is actually placed in the center of the deck. Then fan the deck holding it in the right hand and making the fan with the left fingers. The chosen card still extends beyond the edge of the fan. Now place your left forefinger against the left outer corner of the chosen card and push it into the deck. This action jogs the cards above and below the chosen card at the inner end of the fan.

The procedure thereafter is the same as in the first version.

This sleight gains in effect if it is performed slowly and in an off-hand manner, allowing the spectators to see plainly that the card has been pushed flush into the fan. It can be done best with cards having a fairly rough surface such as Bicycle Air Cushion cards. Most of the cheaper cards are also excellent for the purpose. With highly glazed cards it is necessary to apply more pressure at the inner end of the fan as the card is inserted. It is a good idea to experiment with various brands of cards, for then when you are offered a strange deck you will recognize the texture of the cards and govern your actions accordingly.

More Card Manipulations

SERIES 2

Illustrations by Nelson Hahne

More Card Manipulations No. 2

CONTENTS

More Card Manipulations

No. 2

Part I—SLEIGHTS

THE CURRY TURN-OVER CHANGE

PAUL CURRY

While the actual working of this change bears no resemblance to the Mexican Turn-over, the general effect of the change does; that is the card may be changed either as it is turned face down on the table or as it is turned face up.

The principle behind the sleight is the changing of a card on the table for the bottom card of the deck. The change is made in the act of turning the card face up, or face down, with the hand that holds the deck. In other words, if the pack is held in the left hand and if the card is face up on the table,it would be turned face down by the fingers of the left hand and changed in the action. The card now face down on the table would be the card that was originally on the bottom of the deck, while the card originally face down on the table would become the bottom card of the deck.

METHOD: Hold the cards face down in the left hand as in Fig. 1. Insert the top joint of the third finger above the bottom card and press the top joints of the second and fourth fingers against the ends of this card; thus the bottom card is firmly gripped by the ends of these three fingers and will be turned over by extending them.

The successful accomplishment of the change depends upon the correct position of the deck in the hand. It should be held well down to allow the forefinger to extend well over the outside end. The thumb plays no part in holding the deck, as this is done entirely by second, third and fourth fingers.

Place the card to be changed face up on the table. Bring the left hand to it and rest the tip of the thumb on its right side about half an inch from its outer end, at the same time slip the tip of the forefinger under its left side and raise that side from the table. Fig. 2. Remove the thumb from the card and raise it to a vertical position on its side, holding it between the forefinger and the thumb. Move the hand slightly towards the right and lower the card, now face down, towards the table.

It is at this point that the change takes place. Press the left thumb against the card that is being turned and straighten out the third finger thus pushing out the original bottom card of the deck onto the table. In the meantime the thumb presses up against the original table card and retains it on the bottom of the deck. The entire sleight takes place as the hand moves to the right in the natural action of turning the card over. At first it may be found necessary to press the side of the card against the table to aid the third finger in drawing it from the deck, but with a little practice this help can be dispensed with.

It is hardly necessary to point out that practice will be required to develop the proper coordination of the movements. Properly performed the sleight simulates exactly the mere turning of the card.

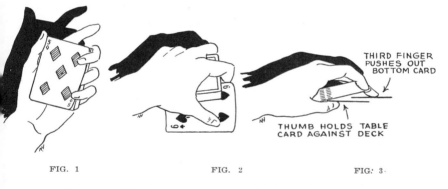

THIRD FINGER
PUSHES OUT
BOTTOM CARD

THUMB HOLDS TABLE
CARD AGAINST DECK

FIG. 1   FIG. 2   FIG. 3

There would be no use for publishing this sleight if it did not have certain advantages over the standard changes now in use. Here are a few examples of how it may be used.

a. Shuffle the pack, then, holding it in the left hand, turn the two top cards as one. Call attention to the face card, say it is the Ace of Spades, turn the two cards face down and deal the top card onto the table. Make the double lift again, this time exposing, say, the Ace of Hearts. Turn these two cards face down and deal the top card, the Ace of Spades, onto the table at some distance to the right of the card (an indifferent card, supposed to be the Ace of Spades) already on the table. Command the cards to change places and with the right hand turn the card on the right face up. It proves to be the

Ace of Spades. With the left hand turn the other card over, executing the change and it proves to be the Ace of Hearts. The cards have obeyed your command.

b. Again, spread the deck face up on the table and invite a spectator to push out any card from the line. Gather up the remainder of the cards and with the left hand turn the selected card face down executing the change for an indifferent card. Spread the pack face down and have the spectator push his card (really an indifferent card) amongst the others. Gather the cards and you have the chosen card on the bottom of the deck to deal with as you please.

c. One more example: Have a card selected, returned, and bring it to the top. After a false shuffle, retaining the card on the top, make the double lift and show, for example, the Ace of Spades, as being the chosen card. The spectator says that card is not his card. Turn the two cards face down and toss the top card carelessly to the table, face down. Shuffle the top card (A.S.) to the bottom and then look through the deck. Pretending to be puzzled about the error, ask the spectator to name his card. He does so and you tell him to turn the card on the table. He turns it face up and acknowledges that it is now his card. With your left hand turn the card face down, executing the change for the Ace of Spades.

Pick this card up as though to put it in the pack, then pause and, as an after thought, ask the spectator what card he thought it was. He replies, "The Ace of Spades." "Quite right," you say, "it is the Ace of Spades" and you turn the card face up.

Other uses for this most ingenious sleight will readily suggest themselves to the experienced performer.

THE "CARLYLE" SNAP DOUBLE LIFT

Here is a most intriguing method of working the double lift by Francis X. Carlyle, whose Four Ace trick in "Card Manipulations No. 5" will be remembered.

It is an ingenious application of the crimp applied to a card lengthways, and is extremely useful in any trick which calls for continuous double lifting. Suppose, for example, in the Ambitious Card trick you have shown that the chosen card has mounted to the top of the deck. Hold the card between the tips of the right thumb and middle finger by the inner corners, the forefinger pressing on the back of the card at the middle of the inner end.   Fig. 4. By pressure of the fingers and thumb bend the card so that its face becomes convex, thus crimping the card lengthways.

FIG. 4

With the left thumb push the top card slightly over the side of the deck, slide the crimped card underneath the top card and square the deck. Grip the inner corners of the deck with the right thumb and second finger and place the tip of the forefinger on the middle of the inner end.   Hold the deck just above the left hand, press downward with the tip of the first finger and riffle the cards off into the left hand, the last two cards will cling to the right thumb and middle finger as one card owing to the crimp in the chosen card. To get the snap effect, let the right hand side of the two cards slip free from the tip of the middle finger and grip them by the opposite corner between the thumb and forefinger.   The side of the cards, thus freed, snaps down on the back of the deck and you immediately lift the two cards and exhibit them as one.

It is surprising how exactly the cards register despite the apparently careless handing.   It is impossible for a spectator to suspect that you hold more than the one card.   In such tricks as The Ambitious Card, Magician versus Gambler, etc., the sleight is invaluable. One enthusiastic correspondent writes "If you use this in the next card book it will justify the book by itself." I would strongly recommend my readers to give the sleight the small amount of practice required to perfect it.

THE JAMISON DOUBLE LIFT

R. M. JAMISON

To vary one's methods is a good rule for the magician to follow. This applies with particular force to the double lift. There are so many fine tricks which require its use several times in succession that it is advisable to have more than one method of lifting two cards as one. Mr. Jamison's sleight is so quick, easy and neat and withal, so illusive, that every card magician should add it to his repertoire of sleights.

METHOD: Hold the deck in the left hand vertically, the backs towards yourself, faces outwards, the left thumb along the upper side, the last three fingers supporting the lower side and the forefinger at the outer end, with the top joint protruding over the top card of the deck. Fig. 5.

Bring the right hand to the deck, the thumb at the inner end, the fingers at the outer end, and with the tip of the right thumb, which is completely covered by the left hand and the deck, separate

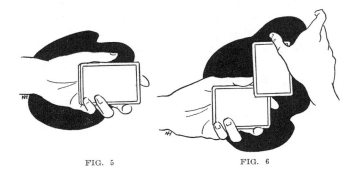

FIG. 5   FIG. 6

the two top cards from the others and press the ball of the thumb against their inner ends. The outer ends of these two cards are thus pressed against the top joint of the left forefinger and they are held by these two digits only.

Now, keeping these two cards parallel with and close to the deck, lever them upwards around the first joint of the left forefinger by moving the right thumb upwards and outwards until the two cards are at right angles to the deck. They are shown thus to the spectator as one card and, without any change of grip, they are levered back to their original position by the reverse action of the right thumb and hand.

As the spectator never gets a glimpse of the edges of the cards, three or more cards can be lifted by this method with perfect safety. Although it would at first seem that their position between the tips of one thumb and one finger must be an insecure one, the fact is that they are more secure from spreading than in any other double lift move.

RIFFLE SHUFFLE CONTROL

ORVILLE MEYER

Used in conjunction with almost any card effect, these moves give the performer perfect control over the chosen card even while proving apparently that the card is utterly lost. If the performer continues with the Hindu shuffle, as explained below, even magicians will be puzzled.

We will suppose that a card has been selected, returned and passed to the top of the pack. (When showing this trick to magicians I merely turn over the top card, asking them to remember it, then turn it face down and preceed to control that card. This is the patter I use in such cases. "Now remember that card. I'll riffle shuffle the pack (1) and you will notice I don't even look at the cards as I shuffle. You can see that they certainly are mixed. (2) The pass, you know, is old fashioned and you notice that I don't use it or hold any breaks anywhere." (3) Remark that you will mix the cards thoroughly. Now continue with the following moves:

1. Divide the deck for a regular riffle shuffle, taking the top half, with the chosen card on top, in the right hand, the lower half in the left hand. Riffle the ends of the halves into each other, dropping the cards in the right hand a little faster so that ten or twelve cards of the left hand packet fall on top at the end of the shuffle.

Begin to push the packets together and then, as is done naturally to facilitate squaring the deck, turn it and hold it in the left hand in about the same position as for dealing, but you have not pushed the two packets flush. The packet that was in the right hand is now nearest to the body; continue pushing the two packets into each other to square the deck, the fingers of the right hand at the outer end and the right thumb at the inner end. It will be seen, therefore, that the right thumb pushes in the packet on top of which is the chosen card. In the action press the fingers and thumb downwards on their respective ends thus curving the deck and raising the inner ends of the ten or twelve indifferent cards above the chosen card. Fig. 7. In the final act of completely squaring the deck, insert the little finger in the break thus made with the result that it holds a break under these few cards and is directly on top of the chosen card. After a trial it will be found that these moves are easily done without looking at the cards at all.

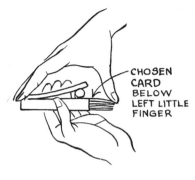

FIG. 7

Such is the riffle control which can be applied to many effects. Magicians, especially, will be puzzled when they realize that an obviously unknown number of cards has been riffled on top of the chosen card. Now, as stated above, when I am showing this to magicians, I follow with the Hindu shuffle and even those familiar with this shuffle will be puzzled further by some of the moves that follow.

2.   The Hindu shuffle follows perfectly here as the left hand is turned slightly to enable the right hand to grasp the pack in the proper position (See Card Manipulations, No. 1, page3). As the hands move apart for the first move of the shuffle, draw off with the left hand the indifferent cards above the little finger. The chosen card is now the top card of those in the right hand. Next, with the left hand, draw off a small packet from the top of the right hand cards, thus the chosen card is now the top card of those in the left hand.

For the third move in the shuffle bring the right hand packet on top of the chosen card, pick up the rear end of that card with the tips of the right third finger and thumb, hold it concealed under the other cards in the right hand, and continue with the regular Hindu shuffle until you have drawn off all the cards above the selected card, then drop it, and any extra cards you may have picked up with it, on the top of the pack.

3. Go right into another Hindu shuffle as follows: As the left hand starts to pull off a packet of cards from the top of the deck, tilt the deck slightly, glimpse the bottom card and remember it. Again, as in the preceding paragraph, when the right hand slaps its cards on the small packet in the left hand, you pick up the chosen card as before, bringing it, of course, right below the glimpsed card. Continue the shuffle until some ten or twelve indifferent cards, the exact number is immaterial, remain in the right hand above the chosen card. Then drop this small packet intact on top of the cards in the left hand actually burying the card in the deck. However, it is not really lost for the card previously glimpsed and remembered is directly above it.

Continue by saying, "You see the card isn't near the bottom," as you turn the deck face up and show several of the bottom cards, "nor is it near the top." Turn the deck face down again, take off half a dozen or so cards from the top, fan them showing their faces and replace them on the **bottom** of the deck. "It really is lost. I don't know **where** it is . . . do you?" As you say these last few words, rapidly turn cards, one by one, face up from the top of the deck, retaining each card in the right hand after showing it. But, although you appear to be absolutely indifferent as to how many cards you turn face up, you are watching for the glimpsed card. As soon as it is turned, place it and all the other cards in the right hand on the bottom of the pack. The chosen card is once more the top card of the deck, awaiting your pleasure.

It would not be good showmanship to reveal the card at this point, so you go into one more regular Hindu shuffle, saying, "Yet I can still shuffle the deck and any time I actually **want** the card, I merely stop shuffling, turn over the top card and there it is."

When you say, "I don't . . . hold any breaks," you have already passed the point where the little finger break is held, and the breaks held in the Hindu shuffle are indetectible, even to the closest observer. While this description is, necessarily, somewhat lengthy, the entire routine takes about sixty seconds and, therefore, can certainly be classed as a snappy effect. I find that the moves in the second paragraph of (3) puzzle even the magicians.

THE RIFFLE LOCATION

The following location will be found very easy to do and quite indetectible. Its original source I have not been able to determine.

Hold a little finger break below the top twelve cards. (You can count these by the left thumb riffle at the top left hand corner of the deck under cover of the right hand as it squares the deck, or you can use the right thumb to riffle off the twelve cards from the bottom and then bring them to the top by the pass or a simple under cut, at the same time securing the little finger break.) Riffle the outer ends of the cards rather slowly and invite a spectator to place his forefinger on any card he pleases as they fall. It is advisable to make the riffle deliberately, not only that all may see that the choice is perfectly free, but also that it may be made before you reach the break below the twelve cards which are above the little finger tip.

Let the spectator remove the card on which he places his finger and the moment he has done so, drop the outer end of the pack a little and cut off the twelve cards with the right hand, the thumb at the inner end of the pack finding the break instantly. The idea is to make it appear that you have cut the deck at the very spot from which the card was taken. This will be taken for granted if you slope the outer end of the pack downward and hold the cut behind the pack and close to your body in an almost vertical position. Be careful not to glance at the right hand, to avoid suspicion of glimpsing the bottom card of the packet in that hand.

Have the spectator replace his card on top of the pack, drop the cut carelessly on the deck keeping the left fingers stretched out and then square the cards very openly. To all appearance the card is completely lost in the pack but you know it is the thirteenth card and you can deal with it in any way necessary for the trick in hand.

The method is a natural for the spelling trick. You have merely to make a false shuffle and several false cuts, have the card named and spell it out in the usual way. The spelling of any card can be faked to take twelve or thirteen letters.

If it is necessary to bring the card to the top of the pack, a simple method is to run six cards into the left hand, drop the rest of the pack on them, shuffle overhand again running six cards, in-jog the seventh and shuffle off. Form a break above the in-jogged card, shuffle to the break and throw the remaining cards on top. The chosen card will then be the top of the deck.

AN EASY BOTTOM DEAL

GERALD KOSKY

The pack is held in the left hand, the thumb along one side, the top joint bent round the outer top corner and the first joints of the four fingers on the other side pressing it against the second joint and the base of the thumb. The pack does not lie flat on the left hand but is raised sufficiently to allow for the insertion underneath it of the right thumb. Fig. 8.

The cards are dealt a card at a time but not in the orthodox manner. Proceed as follows: Place the four fingers of the right hand, held close together, on the top card of the deck, covering it completely, and the right thumb under the deck, draw the top card towards the body and, when it is clear of the deck, turn the hand over and drop card face up on the table.

Continue dealing cards in this way until the bottom card is needed, then, instead of drawing the top card towards the body, draw out the bottom card with your thumb, making exactly the same movements as in dealing the top cards. If the timing and the action in making both the straight and the bottom deal are exactly the same the sleight cannot possibly be detected, regardless of how closely the spectators watch you.

The sleight was shown to me many years ago by one of the cleverest gamblers in the States and has never, to my knowledge, been explained in any book or magazine. It can be used to advantage in many card effects.

FIG. 8

THE NEVER FAIL CARD FORCE

R. M. JAMISON

The following is a method of forcing a card which I have used for years, either for regular cards or Jumbos. It is an ideal method for any magician who balks at any trick that requires the forcing of a card.

At the start the card to be forced is on the top of the deck which is then cut and the portion so cut is placed about three-quarters of an inch inwards that is, near the body, as it lies on the original upper packet, Fig. 9.

As you advance to the "drawee," begin to fan the upper packet, Fig. 10, and just as the spectator is about to reach for a card, start to fan out the lower packet a little, keeping the fan in motion from right to left, so that his finger actually strikes against the force card and, at that moment, you give a trifle more separation at this point to make it easier for him to grasp it. As soon as the card is taken, withdraw the pack towards your body, but continue fanning the lower portion for a moment or two.

FORCE CARD

FIG. 9   FIG. 10

It will be found that the required card is the only one that the spectator can draw out easily and quickly. The fanning operation must be worked as if on a pivot, first your right hand end of the fan is nearest to the spectator, then the center and, finally the left hand end. Although there are really two fans, the operation must make it appear to the spectator that you are offering one large fan of cards.

Once the particular knack of the method is acquired, the force becomes mere child's play. The "drawee" merely follows the path of least resistance by removing a card that offers, perhaps, a little more surface to grasp.

REPLACEMENT OF PALMED CARDS

In No. 1 of this series the replacement of a palmed card, or packet of cards on the pack, which is held in the left hand, was fully explained. The method given there, however, cannot be applied to cases where the palmed cards have to be added imperceptibly to the pack when it is on the table. The best method for this purpose is the following.

Let us suppose that you have a card, or small packet of cards, palmed in the right hand and that a certain number of cards have been counted onto the table by a spectator on your right. The problem is to add the palmed cards to the table packet imperceptibly. Make some such remark as this, "Kindly take these cards in your own hands," and suit the action to the words by momentarily placing your right hand on top of the packet on the table, release the palmed cards and instantly swing the hand upwards, the right thumb, resting on the table at the near side of the packet, acting as a pivot and the fingers being separated. The palm of the hand now empty, is thus brought face towards the spectator with the figers wide apart. Any possible suspicion of palming is nullified. Continue, without a pause, by pushing the cards towards the spectator with the thumb against the side of the packet nearest to you, keeping the hand in the same position. Fig. 11.

The sleight appears to be a very audacious one, but a few trials before a mirror will prove that its very audacity makes it perfectly deceptive.

PALM TOWARD AUDIENCE

FIG. 11

THE VERTICAL PALM

This method of palming has the great advantage that it is executed with the deck held face outwards, the bottom card being visible to the spectators throughout, and under cover of a perfectly natural action.

Stand facing the audience, hold the deck in the left hand, face outwards and vertically on its side, between the first joint of the thumb and the lower index corner and the first joints of the second and third fingers at the opposite outer lower corner; the first finger at the outer end, pressing on the ends of the cards to be palmed, and the little finger free. Fig. 12.

Bring the left hand over the right forearm, nip the sleeve with the left little finger and pull it back a little, as you turn slightly to the right, and show all parts of the right hand.

Swing around to the left in order to pull the left sleeve back with the right hand and, as the right hand passes over the pack, pull the packet to be palmed upwards with the left forefinger, Fig. 13, and catch its top outer corner with the first joint of the right forefinger with that finger press the opposite inner corner of the packet against the base of the right thumb. The packet is thus in a perfect position for palming and you carry it away with the least pause and proceed to pull back the left sleeve.

This palm is very useful in such tricks as "The Cards Up the Sleeve" and in the "Palm and Recovery Flourishes".

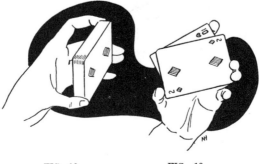

FIG. 12   FIG. 13

THE NEW PACKET CHANGE

The only practical change of one packet of cards for another hitherto known to the profession is the "Hand to Hand Palm Change" explained in "Card Manipulations, No. 2", pages 25 and 26. The sleight I am about to describe is, I think, equally deceptive and easier to do.

We will suppose that you hold a packet of cards, A, openly in the left hand which has to be switched for another packet, B, which you hold palmed in the right hand. Stand with your right side to the audience. Show A fanned, the faces outwards, in the left hand, close the fan with the right hand and turn the packet face down in the left hand, holding it between the thumb on one side and the last three fingers on the other, the left forefinger at the outer end. Fig.. 14.

Raise the left hand showing the cards in this position, then lower it and bring the right hand over the packet A so that the ends of the palmed packet B protrude about an inch, grip both packets by placing the right thumb under A and immediately draw the right fingers down the back of packet B for an inch or so. Hold the packets thus in the right hand which remain stationary, Fig. 15, while you move the left hand away and show all parts of it.

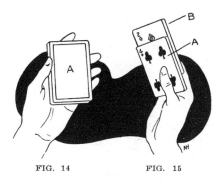

FIG. 14   FIG. 15

Still keeping your right side to the front, bring the hands together, grip the outer end of packet B between the left thumb on one side and the second finger on the other, with the left forefinger push packet A into the right hand which promptly palms it, and move the left hand away with packet B. This packet is now disposed of as may be necessary for the trick and the right hand picks up the deck, adding the palmed packet A to it in the process.

If the action is carried through smoothly the effect to the audience is that the original packet A is not removed from their sight for a moment.

PART II.

SETTING UP POKER HANDS WITH THE RIFFLE SHUFFLE

The enormous publicity recently given to exposures of the method used by cardsharpers makes it highly desirable for every magician to know at least one method of setting up a hand at poker. It is almost certain that club or parlor work, after a display of card tricks, the conversation will turn to these exposures and it is humiliating to have to confess inability to do anything in that line. The two following methods of using a riffle shuffle to set up poker hands have been very kindly supplied to me by Mr. P. W. Miller who is a past master in all wiles of the card table tricksters.

First of all, it is necessary to learn to hold back one, two, three or four cards with either thumb from the top of each packet, prior to actually riffling them together. This is not an easy thing to do and requires some practice. Begin by learning to hold back one card with each thumb and always use the corner riffle, bending the middle of the ends well down with the forefingers and upwards with the thumbs. When you can govern one card with each thumb with ease and certainty, learn to do the same thing with two, three and finally four cards at the top of each packet.

With this sleight at your command it is an easy matter to set threes or two sets of threes.

1. To Run up Three Cards in a Four-Handed Game of Poker

Secretly get three aces to the top of the pack.

Cut by taking the top half of the deck with the left hand, the lower half with the right.

Riffle the packets together, holding back two cards with the left thumb and three cards with the right thumb. At the end of the riffle drop the three cards from the right thumb, then the two cards on them with the left thumb.

Cut as before, top half in left hand, lower half in right.

Riffle again, the left thumb holding back one card, the right thumb three cards, drop the card from the left thumb last.

Cut as before and riffle again. This time the left thumb does not hold back any cards, while the right thumb again retains three and drops them as the last move in the shuffle. The three aces are set to fall to the dealer.

After the first riffle be careful not to run any cards from the right hand packet into the stacked portion of the cards in the left hand.

The number of players, of course, regulates the number of cards to be run between the cards that are being set up.

2. To Set Up Two Hands, Threes in Each Hand, in a Four Hand Game

Secretly get three Kings together on three Aces on the top of the pack.

Cut in the same way as in the first method, the right hand taking the lower half and the left hand the upper half of the pack, but each time you cut, pull the top card of the upper half onto the lower half with the right forefinger.

In the first riffle hold back four cards with the left thumb and three cards with the right thumb, drop the left hand cards last.

In the second riffle hold back two cards with the left thumb and three cards with the right thumb, again dropping the left hand cards last.

In the third and last riffle do not hold back any cards with the left hand and once more hold back three with the right thumb. Drop the three from under the right thumb as the last move in the shuffle.

The two sets will then fall thus, the three Kings to the first man on the left, the three Aces to the dealer. You can, of course, follow the three riffles with an overhand false shuffle and several false cuts.

Once the ability to hold back the required cards is acquired the method will be found very fast and indetectible.

THE BARNYARD SHUFFLE

While this shuffle is primarily a sharper's dodge for setting up hands in a poker or other gambling game, it can be used by the magician to good advantage in making a necessary arrangement under the very noses of the spectators.

The best way for the reader to learn the process will be to take a pack of cards in hand and follow the process move by move. The dealer can run up any kind of a hand for himself, threes, fours, a flush or a full house. We will suppose that you decide to set up a full house of high cards for a five-handed game. Proceed as follows:

Hold the cards in the right hand in position for an overhand shuffle, with the faces of the cards towards the left hand. Begin by running off a few cards into that hand. When a court card or an Ace appears on the face of these cards, throw the whole packet back on the face of the deck. Suppose that the first card to appear is a King. Pick up all the cards that have been run into the left hand thus making the King the bottom card of the deck. Run this card off into the left hand, then pass it to the top of the deck by placing the pack on it and then picking it up with the pack as you continue the shuffle.

Next run off four cards into the left hand, drop the pack on them and pick them up with the pack, thus placing them above the King on the top of the deck. One card has thus been placed in position to come to you in the deal.

Continue the shuffle by running cards into the left hand; suppose the next court card to appear is a Jack. Pick up all the cards in the left hand onto the face of the pack. Pick up all the cards in the left hand onto the face of the pack, making the Jack the face card, pull it off singly, drop the pack on it and so bring it to the top of the deck exactly the same as you did with the King. Run off four cards and send them to the top of the pack as before and you have two cards set up to come to you on the deal.

Continue in the same way, using Kings and Jacks as they happen to come in the shuffle. It may be that you will get three Kings and two Jacks, or three Jacks and two Kings, depending entirely on how the cards come out.

Sometimes when looking for your next court card it may come out as second or third card in the left hand, in such case let these cards go to the top of the pack and then run the difference in number, three cards or two, to make four cards above the court card. If it happens to be the fourth card run off into the left hand, let all four cards go to the top, run off one card and pass that to the top, making four cards on top of the court card. Finally should it be the fifth card you simply pass the whole five cards to the top.

This method of running up a hand is very fast and easy but it requires quick thinking in counting and, of course, practice to accomplish it naturally. As soon as the set up is complete make several false shuffles and false cuts.

Naturally in a gambling game the method can only be used where toying with the deck is allowed, but the magician is under no such restriction. Under cover of a ready flow of patter he can use this Barnyard Shuffle to make any set up he requires, providing, of course, that it is not of too intricate a nature.

I am indebted to Mr. Purvis W. Miller, for the description of this most useful shuffle.

Part III.—TRICKS

A NEW TOP CARD PRODUCTION

After the usual preliminaries of a card having been chosen, returned to the pack and brought to the top by one or the other of the many maneuvers now available, make a false shuffle, leaving the card on the top. Or, if you prefer, you may palm the card and allow a spectator to shuffle the pack, in which case you return the palmed card to the top in the usual way. By means of the double lift show that an indifferent card is on the top.

Place the pack in the left hand, face outwards, as shown in Figure, the thumb lying flat on the upper side of the deck, the first finger at the middle of the outer end and the other three fingers supporting the lower side of the deck. With the tip of the left first finger pull back the end of the top card, at the lower corner, to separate it a little from the other cards. Then push on this corner, first inwards and then upwards, making the card turn between the base of the thumb and the deck until it arrives at a position at right angles to the deck and above it, Figure. The card is then held firmly by pressing the pack against the lower part of the thumb, and the forefinger retakes its position at the outer end of the deck.

This novel and intriguing production is the invention of M. Jules Dhotel, the famous French magician and author.

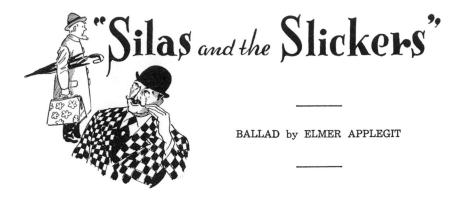

"Silas and the Slickers"

BALLAD by ELMER APPLEGIT

When Silas Green of Pumkinville
　　Prepared to leave the farm,
His father thought some good advice
　　Might do the boy no harm.

"My son," he said, "you're going away
　　To that there distant city.
You're goin' to look for wealth and fame
　　To fail would be a pity.

The city's full of slickers, boy,
　　And crooks and gold brick men,
They'll steal the gold out of your teeth—
　　The ink out of your pen.

Now here's a bit of good advice,
　　You'll find that it is true,
If you will slick the slicker first
　　He can't hornswoggle you."

But Silas, in the great big town,
　　Was seen in evil places—
He met with men who played with cards
　　And girls with painted faces.

Some evil men proposed to Si
　　A little gambling game—
A simple task of matching cards,
　　Stud poker was its name.

The simple rules were soon explained,
  Si should have been on guard,
But recklessly he plunged right in
  And bet on every card.

A crafty gambler dealt the cards,
  A slippery cuss was he.
By crooked dealing he made sure
  Si's first card was a three. (1)

The next card dealt was poorer yet—
  I know it's clear to you:
There's one card lower than a three
  And that card is a TWO. (2)

No quitter, Si put up more cash,
  Thought he, "I'll do and dare."
The next card brightened up the hand
  And Silas had a pair. (3)

So Silas bought another card,
  And Lady Luck seemed kind.
For this card also was a DEUCE——(4)
  He had three of a kind.

The best of things, someone has said,
  Are sometimes out of place;
And Silas found this saying true,
  The next card was an ACE. (5)

The gamboleer who dealt the cards
  Reached out to take the cash,
But Si exclaimed in ringing tones,
  "Stop, Slicker, don't be rash.

We play this game down on the farm
  And in some other places;
And I have found when slickers deal,
  It's well to have FOUR ACES.

The trick depends upon prearrangement, the double lift and false shuffling. On the top of the deck you have the following cards in this order—

Three, Ace, deuce, Ace, deuce, Ace, deuce, Ace, eight cards in all, with the suits in any order.

During the delivery of the first seven verses show the deck and execute several false shuffles, the necessary moves then follow as numbered.

1. Turn the top card, a three, face up on top of the deck and show it. Turn it face down, take it off the top and place it, face outwards, against an inverted tumbler on your table. You have four other inverted tumblers in line with this one, a few inches apart.

2. While speaking this verse execute a false shuffle which will retain the remaining set up cards on the top of the deck. At the word "TWO" make the double lift and turn two cards face up, showing a deuce. Turn the two cards face down, take off the top card, an Ace, and place it, back outwards, against the second glass.

3. While reciting these four lines execute the following false shuffle—with the right hand lift all the cards except the top and bottom cards, leaving them in the left hand. On these two cards drop the upper half of the deck, jog the next card and shuffle off. Form a break at the injog, shuffle to the break and throw the remaining cards on top. At the word "pair" make the double lift and show the second deuce. Complete the sleight, take the top card, an Ace and rest it, face outwards, against the third tumbler.

4. Repeat exactly the same procedure as in 3 and place the third Ace, Back outwards, against the fourth glass.

5. Repeat the false shuffle, getting rid of the deuce and retaining the Ace on the top of the deck. On the word "Ace" turn the top card and show the last Ace. Turn this card face down just as you did in executing the double lift, take it off the deck and place it face outwards against the fifth glass.

The position now is that you have a row of five cards standing upright against the glasses, a Three and an Ace showing, one at each end, and three cards, supposed to be Deuces, between them. At the words "Four Aces" turn these three cards face outwards trimphantly.

It will be noted that the plot of the trick is the same as that in the trick "Magician versus Gambler" in my Annual for 1937. The presentation, however, makes the trick a new one and in the hands of a performer who can deliver the lines effectively a better card feat is hard to imagine.

ANOTHER SPELL

The revelation of a chosen card by spelling its name is always a popular effect. Here is an easy method of dealing with three cards which adds a novel twist to the trick.

EFFECT: Using any deck, the magician has three cards chosen. The pack is shuffled freely after their return and then the first card is spelled out, a card being dealt for each letter in the usual way. Explaining that these feats are done by Magic, the performer spells out that word and the second card appears at the last letter. Then he acknowledges they are accomplished by Sleight of Hand and spells out the three words; the third card appears at the last letter.

METHOD: After a spectator has shuffled the deck, take it from him with your right hand, the thumb on the face of the bottom card, fingers on the top of the pack. With the deck in this position a very slight tilt will enable you to sight the bottom card. Shuffle this card to the top, under-cut about two-thirds of the deck and shuffle off, in-jogging the first card. This action places the sighted card about two-thirds down in the pack with the jogged card immediately above it. Square the cards and insert the tip of the little finger below the jogged card, and, therefore, on top of the known card.

This card must be forced and two other cards freely chosen. You have three chances to force the card and this should be sufficient but if you are doubtful of bringing off the regular force then resort to one of the sure-fire forces, such as the knife force or the handkerchief force. In any case make the most of the free choice of two of the cards.

There are thirteen letters in the words "sleight of hand," so you thumb count twelve cards from the bottom. As you offer the deck for the return of the third card chosen, under-cut the twelve cards, have the card replaced on top of the remainder and openly drop the twelve cards on it, keeping the left fingers extended. False shuffle by under-cutting half the deck, in-jog first card and shuffle off, form break at in-jog, shuffle to break and throw on top. The card is now in the right position to be spelled out, using the words "sleight of hand."

Go to the second spectator, lift off the lower half of the deck in preparation for an overhand shuffle and have his card replaced on the cards in the left hand. Begin an overhand shuffle by running four cards, in-jog the next and shuffle off. Make a break at the in-jog, shuffle to it and throw the remainder on top. Thus the second chosen card becomes the fifth card, ready to be spelled with the word "magic."

For the last card, the forced card, in this case the Eight of Spades which spells with thirteen letters, you thumb count from the bottom twelve cards, draw them out as an under-cut, have the card returned on top of the remainder and drop the twelve cards on top very openly. A final series of false shuffles may now be executed, followed by several false cuts. The position is that the forced card lies thirteenth from the top, the second card is five cards lower down and the third card thirteen cards from that one.

Reveal the first card by spelling its name, dealing one card for each letter in the usual way. Execute a quick false shuffle as you ask the name of the second card, then say in a rather lordly manner, "You know we do these things by MAGIC." Spell the word, dealing a card for each letter, M—A—G—I—C and turn the card on the letter C. Ask the name of the last card and continue in a bantering manner, smiling, "Well, of course you know it's all done by S—L—E—I—G—H—T O—F H—A—N—D," dealing a card for each letter and revealing the chosen card on the last.

TO FLOURISH OR NOT TO FLOURISH?

Robert-Houdin, the great master, set his face strongly against the introduction of flashy flourishes at the beginning of a routine of tricks with cards. He maintained that such a display of digital dexterity must detract from the effect of the tricks which follow. In this he was upheld by Torrini, whose skill with cards has seldom, if ever been equalled. The modern magician thinks otherwise and seldom misses any opportunity of showing his cleverness by making fans, arm spreads and catches, the back and front palm and so on, indeed card manipulators make a complete act of such flourishes.

The question then arises, why not incorporate these flourishes in a card trick, properly so-called. The following arrangement is a set trick which allows for the introduction of such flourishes as the operator is most adept with, in a very appropriate manner, the whole being made interesting and entertaining by pattering on the subject of the coincidences between a deck of cards and an almanac. It necessitates a prearrangement as follows—

12 court cards, x x x 4 x x x x x x 7 s . . . Ace. x denotes any indifferent card, the sixteenth card is a four of any suit, the twenty-third card is the seven of Spades and the last card of the deck is any Ace but the Ace of Spades. Reference to page 23 will show how this simple arrangement can be made under the very eyes of the spectators.

To present the trick, begin by making a false shuffle, then with the right thumb break the inner end of the deck at the seven of Spades and insert the tip of the left little finger to hold a break at that spot. Very little practice will enable you to break the pack at the right spot or within a card or two. Cover the action by riffling the inner ends with the right thumb. Advance to a spectator and have a card selected by having him insert his forefinger as you riffle the outer ends of the cards. Do this rather slowly so that a choice will be made before you reach the break held by the left little finger. As soon as the spectator has removed his card, cut the pack at the break, making it appear that you cut at the very spot from which the card was removed.

Invite the spectator to show his card to the rest of the audience, have it replaced on the cards in your left hand, then drop the cut (the twenty-three prearranged cards) on top, very openly and with the left fingers extended. Square the pack and say—

"It is popularly supposed that cards were invented to amuse the mad King Charles VI of France, but in reality they have a much more ancient origin than that. The story arose from the fact that records were discovered that the Court painter, Gringgoneur, received a very large sum for painting cards for that monarch. Let me illustrate that."

Make the reverse fan showing the cards all blank and keep the left little finger covering the Ace spot on the face card. "You see the cards are all blanks." Close the fan and make a very wide regular fan, keeping the backs of the cards to the front by turning slightly to the left. "When I want to restore the faces I simply blow on the cards and you see the results." Blow on the cards and turn their faces to the front. Display them, then square the deck.

"It is not generally known," you continue, "that a pack of cards makes a good substitute for an almanac. For example there are fifty-

two weeks in a year and fifty-two cards in a deck. I'll count them."
Hold the deck face down by the inner end, well in the fork of the
thumb and riffle the outer ends loudly with the middle finger of the right
hand. "Fifty-two exactly. You don't believe that I counted them? I'll
tell you the secret. You let the cards go in bunches of five like this."
Do this, let five cards escape from the middle finger, pause, then
another five, pause and another five, then riffle off the remainder very
rapidly, pretending to count. "It's just a matter of practice. Theatre
treasurers count their stubs the same way, just as quickly and never make
a mistake.

"Again, there are 365 days in the year and the total values of all
the cards in a deck total 365. Here's another way of counting when it
is necessary to see the faces of the cards." Spring the cards, faces
upwards, to the widest extent you are capable of and bring the left
hand up against the right with a bang. "Three hundred an sixty-
four," you exclaim, "I must have missed an Ace. Let's try again"
Make the spring flourish again. "Still I get 364 only. Oh, of course,
the Joker counts as one and I removed that card before beginning the
trick."

Run through the faces of the cards as if to verify this and insert the tip of the left little finger under the last court card. Square
the cards with the faces outwards and palm the twelve court cards
in the right hand by means of the method on p. 130, "Card Manipulations No. 5". Hold the pack also in the right hand for a moment
then put it in the left hand and point to it with the right forefinger
as you continue. "'There are twelve months in the year and twelve court
cards in the pack." Riffle the outer left corner of the deck with the
left thumb and look down at your right knee. "There they go. Did
you see them?" Drop the right hand behind the knee and produce the
palmed court cards in a fan. Spread them as widely as possible as you
say, "Just twelve, no more, no less."

Place these twelve cards on the bottom of the deck.

"There's no end to these curious coincidences. For instance,
there are four seasons in the year. I deal off three cards and turn
the next one, a four. It always happens so. Why I don't know." Put
these four cards on the bottom.

"Again, there are seven days in the week. I deal six cards so and
the seventh card is a seven. It has to be. It can't help itself." Drop
the deck on these seven cards and take the whole deck in your hands
again.

"Just one more curious fact. There is one extra day in Leap Year and your card," address the spectator who chose a card, "will leap at the opportunity of representing it. What was your card? The .... of .... ? Very well. Watch." Drop the deck on the table and the chosen card which, owing to the successive removals of the cards above it, is now at the top, turns over face upwards.

While this method of producing the card is effective, it has become rather widely known and it would be better to adopt the new top card production. Page 25.

It will be noted that the operator can substitute arm spreads for the spring flourishes, various fans with the backs of the cards to the spectators, particularly when using cards with brightly colored backs, also color changes, in fact, while retaining the main idea, the performer can adapt the trick to his own idiosyncracies.

POKER HAND REPEAT TRICK

The following trick was inspired by the very popular trick "The Six Cards Repeat" by Tommy Tucker. In effect, cards are taken from the deck and counted as five. Two cards are thrown on the table and the remainder again counted as five. This process is repeated four times, so that after eight have been discarded there are still five which on being turned face up, prove to be a Royal Flush of Spades. The patter runs to the effect that once when playing a game of poker with a gambler the operator suspected him of having dealt extra cards to his own hand and challenges him to that effect. The hand is counted and proves to consist of five cards only.

Then he suspects the gambler of having slipped two cards into his sleeve, and two cards are dealt off onto the table to illustrate the action. Again the hand is counted—five cards only.

Again he accuses the gambler of pocketing two cards, and two more cards are thrown out, but when the hand is counted it is proved to be quite regular, five cards and five only. Twice more the gambler is challenged and each time two cards are put from the hand to the table, but each time a count proves that there are only five cards in the hand.

Finally, in disgust, the hand is called and it proves to be a Royal Flush of Spades.

The set up required consists of thirteen cards as follows—

X JS 10S X X X QS X X KS AS X X

The packet is bridged lengthways and placed on the top of the deck

To begin the trick, take the bridged packet off the deck, hold it in the left hand as for the glide and proceed to count the cards as five. To do this, glide the bottom card back a little, draw off the top card with the right thumb onto the right fingers, counting "One"; draw off the next card in the same way, letting it fall on top of the first, and count "Two"; draw off another and count "Three"; draw off all the rest except the bottom card, **as one card,** and count "Four"; then snap the last card with the first finger and thumb, plainly showing it is a single card and take it on top of the others in the right hand, counting "Five". Following the patter throw the two top cards onto the table.

Count the cards a second time in exactly the same way and again throw down the two top cards.

The same procedure is carried through a third and a fourth time, eight cards in all being discarded and a final count, in the same way, shows that there are just five cards in the hand and when these are turned face up they prove to be the Ace, King, Queen, Jack and ten of Spades.

This ingenuous arrangement is by Mr. P. W. Miller.

MENE, TEKEL, UPHARSIN

The ever popular trick of passing a number of cards from one spectator's pocket into that of another, was first explained by Robert-Houdin in his book "The Secrets of Conjuring and Magic", (still the best textbook on the art of magic). Many different methods of working the trick have been devised but the procedure which follows has several novel features which have not yet been published.

EFFECT: Any deck may be used and a spectator, A, counts off thirty cards from it, the remainder being put aside. He cuts the pack of thirty cards into two portions. The second spectator, B, chooses one of these, picks it up and places it in his pocket. The remaining packet is counted, we will suppose there are fourteen cards and these cards A places in his pocket after noting the top and bottom cards. B therefore, has sixteen cards.

Three cards are ordered to pass from B's pocket to A's.

B's cards are counted, he has thirteen only.

A's cards are counted, he now has seventeen and he finds that the top and bottom cards are the cards he previously noted.

Again the packets are pocketed and two cards are ordered to pass across. On the recount B has eleven cards and A has nineteen and the cards he noted are still in position at the top and bottom of his packet.

WORKING: Invite two spectators to come forward and place one, A, on your right, the other, B, on your left. Hand the deck to A and instruct him to count off thirty cards and hand you the remainder. These cards you give to B to put in his trousers pocket.

Take the thirty cards from A to verify the number and deal them one by one on the table, counting aloud. Stack the cards neatly until you reach the twenty-eighth which you place slightly overlapping the others to the right. Pick up the cards, square them, slip the tip of the little finger under the side of the protruding card and palm the three top cards in the right hand as you put the packet on the table.

Ask A to cut off about half the cards and to hold the cards he takes. Invite B to pick up the remainder and place them in his coat pocket. Now say that it is necessary for everyone to know how the cards are divided and have A count his cards slowly, one by one, letting them drop from a height of about a foot, onto the table. In this way the cards will make an uneven packet, this facilitating the operation you now have to do. We will suppose there are fourteen cards, as the last card drops place your right hand on the packet, release the three cards from the palm and instantly turn the hand upwards and outwards, using the thumb as a pivot and with the thumb push the cards towards A. (See Replacement of cards, p. 17.)

Instruct A to take the fourteen cards (really seventeen) and place them in his coat pocket, after noting the top and bottom cards of the packet. This done, turn to B . . . . "We had thirty cards. Our friend here has taken fourteen, how many have you in your pocket? Sixteen? Right at the first guess. Now I propose to send three cards across from one packet to the other." Turn to A, "I can take them from yours and send them across this way," pointing to B, "but perhaps it will be better to send them the other way as this gentleman's cards (B's) have not been touched since the cards were counted. It is simply a matter of will power and if you all help me by willing the cards to go, there will be no difficulty in the matter. All ready? One, Two, Three, Go."

Address B, "Will you take out your cards and count them on the table one by one so that all can follow the count? You had how many? Sixteen? Right. Now you have thirteen only. Three cards have left your packet." As you say this gather the cards, palm off two, and hand the remainder back to B, telling him to put them in his pocket, to keep them safe until the other packet is counted.

Have A take his cards from his pocket and count them as before. When he reaches the fourteenth card, stop him by placing your right hand on top of the counted cards and add the two palmed cards in pushing the packet slightly as before. Do this as if merely to draw

special attention to the last three cards which you count aloud . . . .
"Fifteen, sixteen, seventeen. You had fourteen, I sent you three, making
the seventeen which you now have. Will you look at the top and
bottom cards? They are the same? Thank you.

"Although it will be extraordinarily difficult, I will try to experiment again. This time I will send two cards only across the same
way and you will note that I do not touch either packet. One, Two,
Go."

B counts his cards and finds he has ten only. A counts his and
finds he has twenty. Again he notes the top and bottom cards of his
packet and certifies that they are still the same cards.

Smoothly done the trick has an extraordinary effect and it is
still one of the best impromptu tricks with cards that it is possible
to perform.

The spectator will generally forget about the cards he has in his
trousers pocket, so when he reaches his seat you call him back and
ask for them, thus garnering another laugh.

LOST AND FOUND
PAUL CURRY

This is a very surprising trick in which Mr. Curry's change plays
an indispensable part.

EFFECT: Two spectators are asked to each think of a number
and note the cards that appear at those numbers. The pack is shuffled
and to prove the shuffle has been a genuine one it is shown that neither
of the cards now lie at the number thought of. A third spectator pushes
these two indifferent cards, reversed, into the deck at different points.
The two cards thought of are now named and they are found to lie
below the reversed cards, one beneath each.

WORKING: Invite a spectator to think of a number between
one and ten, then you deal ten cards face up and request him to note
the card that appears at his number. Turn to a second spectator
and ask him to think of a number between ten and twenty, then to
note at what number his card lies as you continue the count up to
twenty in dealing ten more cards. Pick up the twenty cards and replace
them on the top of the deck.

Proceed now with an overhand shuffle, under-cut about half the
pack, run one card, in-jog the next card and shuffle off: make a break
at the in-jog, shuffle to the break and throw the remaining cards on
top. The original top twenty cards are again on the top in the same
order with one card above them, thus placing the cards thought of
one card lower down in each instant. Ask the first spectator what

number he thought of and deal cards rapidly, face down, to one less than the number named. Take the top card in your right hand and drop the rest of the pack on top of the cards just dealt. Show the card to the spectator who says that it is not his card and you put it aside face down.

Take the pack again and continuing the count from where you left off with the first person, show that the card at his number is also an indifferent one, place it aside with the first one and drop the remaining cards on those dealt on the table. The process has placed the first card thought of at the bottom and the second one on the top. Execute a quick shuffle bringing the bottom card to join the other selected card at the top.

This business of showing the cards at the spectators' numbers should be done rapidly and carelessly as though not at all important but merely to convince everyone that you shuffled thoroughly.

Announce that it is quite impossible for you to find the cards that were thought of so you will have a spectator do it for you. Pick up one of the two cards on the table and place it face up on top of the pack. Square the deck and with the right thumb raise some six or seven cards slightly and, in turning the pack face up, make the Herrmann pass, transferring these cards to the bottom. Drop the pack, now face up, on the remaining face down cards on the table, then pick it up and turn it over showing this card faced on the top. Apparently there are now two face up cards on the top, in reality there is but one, the other being somewhere near the bottom above the two thought of cards.

Hand the deck to a third spectator to put behind his back. "Of course I'm only guessing," you remark, "but I think that one of the cards is somewhere above the middle of the deck, so suppose you push the ——— of ——— (the top reversed card) into the pack a little above the center." When this has been done, you smile and say, "That's fine. I believe you put the card just where I wanted it. I think the other card is somewhere near the bottom so suppose you push the ——— (pause as though you had forgotten the name of the second reversed card, step to the side of the spectator, glance at the pack behind him and name the second reversed card. This is mere byplay for the card is in the pack near the bottom.) ——— of ——— into the pack down near the bottom."

Watch the spectator closely and when you judged that he has begun to insert his card, exclaim, "Just a moment, please. You haven't pushed the card home yet? No? I'm afraid you were pushing it in too far down. Put it a little higher in the pack." This is more byplay but it eliminates the possibility of the spectator pushing the card amongst the reversed and selected cards near the bottom.

Have the pack brought forward, take it and fan the cards until the first reversed card shows up. Cut the pack at this point, leaving the reversed card on the bottom and deal the first card, face down, on the table. Run through the cards again and cut the second reversed card to the bottom. The two cards thought of are now on the top of the deck. Deal the top card face down on the table to the right of the first card. Ask the spectators to name their cards as you quietly insert the third finger of the left hand under the top card in preparation for the Turn-over change. When the cards have been named turn over the card on the right with the right hand and the card on the left with the left hand executing the change for the top card. The two cards, merely thought of, are now face up on the table.

It will be noted that the first part of the trick is taken from Paul Rosini's excellent trick explained on page 256 of "Greater Magic."

A TWO PILE MYSTERY

FRED BRAUE

This fine trick was originated by Mr. Braue and was sent to me for inclusion in this series soon after the appearance of "More Card Manipulations No. 1." It has, in the meantime, been credited to other performers.

To begin with you hand the deck to a spectator to shuffle to his own satisfaction. Invite him to think of any number between one and ten. Turn away and instruct him to deal two piles of cards to the number of which he is thinking. Let him, A, take one packet and a second spectator, B, take the other. Ask each of them to note the bottom card of his packet, and B then covers his packet with both hands hiding it so that you have no chance of making an estimate of the number of the cards he holds. Instruct A to put his packet on the top of the pack, square the cards and hand the pack to you.

Execute a false shuffle and while pattering idly deal eleven cards face down on the table, thus reversing their order. "On second thought," you say, "I'll use both packets at the same time." Replace the eleven cards on the pack, at the same time noting the bottom card as a key card. Turn away and have B replace his packet on the top and carefully square the cards.

Take the pack and again make a false shuffle. A's card will now be the twelfth card from the top. Have it named and spell it out, faking the spelling if necessary. Place this card aside, leaving the eleven cards on the table before you.

Turn the pack with the faces of the cards towards you and count the cards to, and including, the key card. Suppose it lies sixth, subtract six from eleven, result five, and you know that the second card, B's, will be the fifth card in the packet of eleven lying on the table. This card, therefore, you can produce in any manner you please.

Finally you can divine the number originally thought of by simply adding one to the number at which the key card lies. In this case the number thought of would be seven.

A most impressive and bewildering trick and a fine addition to the magician's stock of impromptu card tricks.

NAME YOUR NUMBER

NEWTON HALL

EFFECT: A card having been freely selected by a spectator, noted by him and returned to the deck, the pack is shuffled. The chosen card is then passed to any number in the deck that the spectator chooses.

METHOD: Any deck may be used, a borrowed one if you wish. Invite a spectator to shuffle the cards, retain one and return the deck to you. When he has noted his card have it returned to the deck, control it by your favorite method (two indetectible methods will be found in the section devoted to sleights), and after shuffles and cuts, to taste, leave the card on the top.

It is then optional whether you palm the card and allow the spectator to shuffle, or go right ahead with the trick. If you have mastered the one hand top palm and the replacement of a palmed card, their use certainly makes the trick stronger.

In either case, with the card on the top of the pack, invite the spectator to name any number at which he would like his card to appear. We will suppose he answers, "Ninth". Riffle the cards and order the card to go to that number, then, holding the pack in the left hand as for dealing, push off the top card and take it, face down, in the right hand, counting "One". Push off the next card and take it with the right hand underneath the first card, counting "Two". Proceed in the same way, handling the cards openly and deliberately, until you have taken off eight cards, each one going below the others in the right hand, so that the chosen card remains the top card of the packet. At the count of "Nine" push the card off the pack as before, but place it on top of the packet in the right hand, making the chosen card the second card of the packet of nine. Replace these cards on the top of the deck and square up.

"Now," you say, "we have the ninth card on the top of the pack and, if my trick has succeeded, it should be your card. Please name it." In the meantime you have separated the two top cards and pushed them, as one card, halfway over the side of the deck. The moment the card is named, turn the left hand over bringing the pack face up over the right hand, held palm downwards, pull the top card back onto the deck with the left thumb and with the tips of the two middle fingers of the same hand, push the second card, face up, onto the palm of the right hand. Instantly bend the top joint of the right second finger under the outer end of the card, nip it between this finger and the tips of the first and third fingers, Fig., straighten the fingers and present the card, face out, towards the spectator, as you say, "Your card, sir."

An alternative presentation is this: Instead of having the spectator choose a number, claim that you have already placed the card at a certain number from the top of the dack and that you will transmit that number to the subconscious mind of the spectator and cause him to name that very number. Whatever number he calls, you assert that it is the number you willed him to name and you proceed to prove it.

SIMULTANEOUS MAGIC

We have had simultaneous chess, simultaneous checkers, and so on, but simultaneous magic should be something of a novelty. The trick that follows entails some trouble but the effect is well worth the pains taken to bring it about.

EFFECT: The performer and three other persons seat themselves at a bridge table, each takes a new deck, merely thinks of one card, and then mixes the cards by dealing them into five heaps and reassembling them. Each person then spells out the name of the card he has thought of, in the usual way, dealing one cards for each letter and placing the card that follows the last letter face downward. In all four cases these cards prove to be the very cards mentally chosen.

PREPARATION: Four new packs are required. Open them by steaming off the seals and arrange the first six cards of each pack as follows:

Pack No. 1.	A C,	2 H,	4 S,	Q S,	4 D,	Q D.
Pack No. 2.	2 C,	6 S,	K H,	8 H,	K D,	8 D.
Pack No. 3.	10 C,	A H,	5 S,	3 H,	9 D,	3 D.
Pack No. 4.	6 C,	10 S,	9 S,	7 H,	5 D,	7 D.

Note that the first card of each set spells with ten letters, the next with eleven letters, and so on, up to the last which spells with fifteen. Shuffle the remaining cards of each pack, place the four sets of six cards on top of their respective packs, replace the packs in their cases, affix the seals and, if you can make a neat job of it, cover them with cellophane. You are then ready to do the trick.

METHOD: Produce the four packs and invite three persons to sit with you around a bridge table. Call attention to the packs still in the regulation wrappers and with the seals intact. Remove the packs from the cases one by one, false shuffling each pack and laying them in turn, one pack before each person, and the last in front of yourself, laying stress on the fact that everything must be done simultaneously and in unison, therefore the cards must not be touched until all are ready.

This done, invite the three players to each think of a small number from one to six, saying that you will do the same. Next instruct them to deal six cards face up in a pile before them and note as they do so which card is at the number they have mentally chosen. Impress on them to deal slowly and regularly, in time with you, so that there can be no possible indication as to when their numbers are reached. Deal your six cards deliberately, think of one of them and see that the others deal six cards and only six.

Pause a moment and impress on each person that he is to fix his thoughts on the card that was his number. Say that you will have all the cards thoroughly mixed and have each person do exactly as you do. Again impress upon each the idea of unison, so that the experiment will not fail and so on. Deal one card face up to the left of

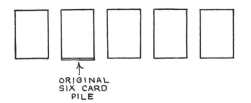

ORIGINAL
SIX CARD
PILE

your pile of six cards, the others doing the same with their cards, then a card on the pile of six, then three cards separately to the right of the six pile. See that they deal card for card with you.

This done, deal a card on the one to the left of the original pile, then one on that pile and one on each of the other three cards to the right. Continue in the same way exactly until the pack is exhausted, the last card falling on the packet to the extreme left. Insist throughout that the others keep exact time with you in dealing. You will not only get some fun out of this, trying to get all three to deal with clockwork precision, but will distract attention from the method you are using to make them actually set up their cards.

Collect your piles, the others doing the same in unison, by picking up the one at the extreme right, putting this one on the next pile, these two on the third, these three on top of the second and all four on top of the extreme left pile. The packs, having thus been reassembled are turned face down in unison and held ready for dealing. Instruct each player that he is to spell mentally, the card of which he is thinking and to deal one card face down on the table for each letter. Explain this thoroughly, especially the use of the word "of", and that when the last letter of the name of the card is reached, each one is to place the next card face down on the table by itself. You do this with the card you remembered and the others will follow suit.

Remark about the curious results that are obtained when four people keep their minds and actions in exact unison. You say, "Now I thought of the ———— of ———— I have done exactly the same as you and you see, in spite of the thorough mixing of the cards, here is the very card I thought of," and you turn your card face up.

"Remember," you continue, "that, from first to last, each of you has had his cards in his own possession. No one else has touched them." Turn to the man on your left, "will you name the card you thought of? The ———— of ————? Kindly turn your card over." Proceed in the same way with the man opposite you and finally with the man on your right.

The result is astonishing to say the least.

THE "LAST WORD" LOCATION

O. W. MEYER

The principle utilized herein is an old one, but the method of handling is new. It is only necessary that you know the top and bottom cards of the deck. Probably the best method of acquiring this knowledge imperceptibly is the well known one of glimsing at the bottom card after an overhand shuffle. In making a second overhand shuffle bring this glimpsed card to the top and glimpse the new bottom card. A false cut may now be made, if desired—an especially practical and deceptive one for this trick is explained in "Card Manipulations No. 3", page 70. Should a magician-spectator suspect that you know the top card, the use of the two key cards and the procedures that follow, will puzzle him.

Place the pack on the table and invite a spectator to cut it into three piles. As he does this note where the top and bottom portions lie. Lay stress on the fact that the cuts are made at random and then invite him to look at the top card of any of the three piles, or the bottom card of any of the three piles, which ever he desires. This done, proceed as follows—

1. If he looks at the top card which you know, or the bottom card which you know, you are set for a real miracle, for you can then allow him to replace it anywhere and give the pack all the shuffling he wishes. Knowing the card you can produce in any way you may prefer.

2. If, however, he looks at one of the two top or bottom cards that you do not know, ask him to remove it and lay it, face down, in

front of the three piles. Then have him place any one of the three piles on top of it.

a. If he places the pile, the bottom card of which you know, on top of his card, you are all set for now his card is next to your known key card and he can replace the other packets in any order and give the whole pack several cuts, still you can easily locate his card as it is under the one you know.

b. If he places the pile containing the top card which you know on his card, ask him to give this packet a complete cut. This brings his card above your top card and you continue as in the preceding paragraph.

c. If, however, he places the pile which has neither of the key cards on his card, continue by asking him to place another pile on this. If this second pile is the one with the known top card have him give the packet a complete cut at this point and continue as in paragraph b.

d. If, for the second pile, he takes one with the known bottom card, simply forget all about this bottom key card, have him continue by placing the third and last pile on top of all and give the pack a complete cut. Again this card is brought next to the card you know.

In all cases, the ultimate result is always practically the same and the spectator's card will be next to a card you know. You are ready then to reveal the chosen card as dramatically as possible. As this is a location idea I will give only one method of revealing the card, others will readily suggest themselves.

Ribbon spread the card, faces upwards, on the table. Then patter along these lines . . . "Your card was a red card . . . Yes . . . it is a Heart . . . an odd Heart . . ." At this point push some odd Heart forward, not the selected card, and they will think for the moment that you have missed, then continue, "Yes, it was the Five of Hearts."

The procedure is the acme of subtlety. With this location I have puzzled many well informed magicians. One trial will prove how utterly baffling it is, even to the closest watcher, because of its apparent haphazardness. Another good feature of the method is the fact that there is no tiresome or attention-distracting "dealing cards until you wish to stop," etc. The routine is direct and to the point, with no padding.

AGAIN THE INFALLIBLE PREDICTION

This trick by Audley V. Walsh and Hal Haber, which first appeared in the No. 1 of this series, has had a most favorable reception and has impelled quite a number of correspondents to offer variations in the working. Of these I have selected two by Orville Meyer. In his methods the full deck of fifty-two cards is used and the necessity of palming off two cards at the start and returning them to the pack, is thereby avoided.

METHOD No. 1. Sight the bottom card as in the original trick and write the prediction accordingly. The spectator then counts off **twelve cards** onto the table and from these he places four in line face upwards. The remaining eight are placed below the remainder of the deck. The routine then continues in the same way as before, the spectator deals cards onto each of the four face up cards to make a total of ten. The four packets of cards thus dealt are gathered up and the remainder of the deck placed on top of them. The spots of the four faced cards are added together and the spectator deals cards to correspond with the total, the last card being placed aside face down.

The prediction is read and the card turned up, they correspond.

On the repetition of the trick, count off twenty-two cards instead of twelve, three of these are placed face up and the working is continued as described above.

METHOD No. 2. If the identity of the card third from the bottom is known, the trick may then proceed exactly as in the original version using ten cards the first time and twenty cards for the repetition. This card may be glimpsed by making a quick fan or a known card may be placed in the desired position by a quick shuffle. However, as a strong feature of the trick is the fact that the performer does not touch the pack after handing it to the spectator to shuffle, an opportunity of sighting the third card from the bottom can be made by having him spread the cards face up either to show everyone that they are thoroughly mixed, or to make sure that the Joker is not amongst them.

Either of these methods, but particularly the second, will serve to throw a fellow magician, who might be conversant with the original trick, completely off the track.

In the current "Magician Monthly" (That invaluable sixpennys-worth of magic) still another version of this prediction effect appears, a contribution by Peter Warlock. In this case, however, the operator must handle the cards, but on the other hand he does not have to glimpse any card after the deck has been shuffled by the spectator. The effect is that the magician writes a prediction, then any full deck is shuffled by a spectator, who takes any card he pleases, a six-spot, for example, puts it face down and deals cards on it to make a total of twelve, that is, he deals six cards on the six-spot. He takes a second card, a deuce, for instance, lays it face down, apart from the first packet, and on it deals ten cards, again making a total of twelve. Two more packets are made in the same way. If a court card is put down, its value is taken as ten.

The four packets are turned over, the spots on the bottom card are totalled and the pack is assembled, a rubber band being placed around it. The prediction is read, the cards are dealt to the number arrived at by adding the values of the four bottom cards, and that card is turned face up. It is the very card foretold.

METHOD: Palm a card, sight it in laying the deck on the table, reach into your trousers pocket for a pencil stub and leave the card in the pocket. Write the name of this card on a slip of paper, fold it and hand it to a spectator to place in his pocket.

Invite a spectator to shuffle the deck to his own satisfaction and then select any card, we will suppose he takes a six-spot, lay it face down on the table and deal on it, face down, as many cards as will bring the total to twelve. In this case, therefore, he must deal six cards. This same operation is repeated three times, making four packets in all.

In the meantime you have had ample opportunity to palm the pocketed card in your right hand. By way of showing what you want the spectator to do, pick up the first heap, secretly adding the palmed card to it, turn it face up so that the value of the bottom card can be noted. Instruct the spectator to turn the second heap, note the value of the bottom card, add it to that of the bottom card of the first heap and place the packet on top of the first, both being face up. He does the same with the remaining two heaps and makes a note of the total thus arrived at. The resulting pile is turned face down, thus making the card you added the top card, and the remaining cards of the deck are placed on top of it.

Have a rubber band placed around the deck and your prediction is brought out and read. The spectator deals cards to the number he noted and turns up the last card. It is the card you predicted.

By using this method first and then repeating the trick by one of the preceding methods in which you do not handle the deck at all, the mystery becomes absolutely unfathomable.

PART IV.

NEW MANIPULATIONS

JOSEPH COTTONE

a. The "Cottone" Squeeze Production

1. Here is a method of card production right off the beaten track. Instead of being produced at the tips of the fingers the card appears at the top of the clenched hand, its lower left corner clipped by the tip of the forefinger bent in against its base. Fig 1.

To produce this effect, hold the deck in the left hand, upright, between the thumb on one side, and the fingers on the other, the bottom card facing the spectators.

Stand with your right side to the front.

Pat the top of the deck with the fingers of the right hand as though merely to square the cards, at the same time push the top (rearmost) card into the fork of the right thumb with the left forefinger. Fig. 2.

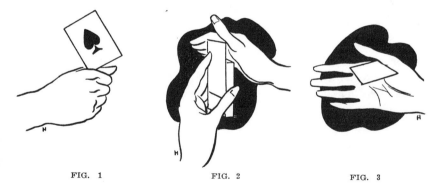

FIG. 1   FIG. 2   FIG. 3

Raise the right hand clear of the pack with the back of the hand towards the front and the top of the hand tipped slightly forward, the card being clipped by an index corner in the fold at the base of the thumb extending outwards almost at a right angle to the palm of the hand. The slight tilt of the hand causes the card to be completely hidden by the palm. The first joint of the thumb should be separated from the side of the hand and only the base pressed in. Fig. 3.

To produce the palmed card, open the fingers as widely apart as possible then bend them inwards in succession, beginning with the little finger, in the following manner: Put the tip of the little finger on the lower end of the card at the inner corner, slightly relax the pressure of the thumb and push the card upwards about half an inch, then place the tip of the third finger against the edge of the bottom

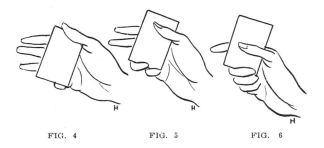

FIG. 4   FIG. 5   FIG. 6

of the card and slide it along, thus continuing the motion of the card upwards; follow this with exactly the same movements with the second finger and the first finger, each of the four fingers closes on the palm in turn and each one pushes the card up further until the closing of the first finger clips the lower right hand corner leaving the card in full view above the fist. Figs. 4, 5, 6, and 1.

The production is made under cover of an upward and outward swing of the hand to the left. The card is literally squeezed out of the hand by the action of the fingers closing in succession. With practice the production can be made in an instant.

The first card having been produced, the next process is the stealing of the second card. Keeping the first card in the same position, push it partly into the deck, Fig. 7, then push it in flush with the rest and pat the top of the deck as before, the left forefinger pushing the rearmost card into the fork of the right thumb. This card is then caught as explained above.

A second method of replacing the card caught from the air and stealing another card is this: turn the card sideways from its position in Fig. 8 and take the opposite corner between the tips of the thumb and first finger with the palm of the hand to the front. Push it down into the pack, and as soon as it is flush, turn the hand bringing its back to the front, clipping the card pushed up by the left forefinger at that precise moment, Fig. 9, and move the hand away, ready to repeat the production.

FIG. 7   FIG. 8

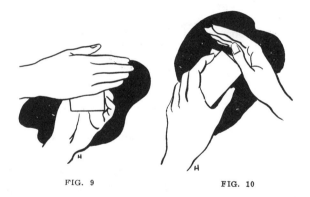

FIG. 9   FIG. 10

After two or three cards have been produced by the use of this steal of a single card, and the last one is pushed into the deck, separate a packet of ten or twelve cards at the back of the deck with the tip of the left forefinger. Push them towards the right, Fig. 10, so that the top right corner protrudes, and clip this corner of the packet in the right thumb crotch in the same way as for a single card. This whole packet is then slid through the right hand and produced **as one card** in just the same way as for a single card.

The knack of keeping the packet of cards together evenly as one card can only be acquired by practice. The best way is to begin with only three or four cards and keep adding more until you can slide a packet of twelve cards or more evenly through the fist.

Having produced the packet as one card at the top of the fist, lay the rest of the pack on the table, seize the lower outer corner of the packet between the tip of the left thumb and first and second fingers, Fig. 11, open the right hand and clip the top index corner of the packet in the thumb crotch as the left hand draws away the **face** card and shows it. Fig. 12. Drop the right hand a little as the left hand tosses away its card, then continue the production in the same way until the packet is exhausted.

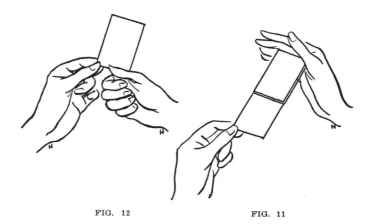

FIG. 12   FIG. 11

b. The "Cottone" Snap Production

Clip a packet of some dozen or more cards, face outwards in the right hand between the top joints of the last three fingers, the tips of the second and fourth fingers being on the face of the packet, that of the third behind it, the first finger extended and the thumb slightly separated from the side of the hand, Fig. 1. The back of the hand being towards the front, the cards are completely hidden from the view of the audience by the hand itself and the top of the wrist.

To produce the cards one by one from this position, turn the hand so that the forefinger points towards the floor, Fig. 2. Swing the packet a little outwards by slightly extending the last three fingers and press the tip of the thumb on the back of the top card, freeing it and pushing it towards the left. Seize it between the tips of the thumb and forefinger, stretching them out to full length, Fig. 3, and let the remainder of the packet snap back into its first position against the palm of the hand. The sound thus produced will be found to heighten the effect of the production of each card. Proceed in the same way until the packet is exhausted. The free ends of the packet should always point towards your body.

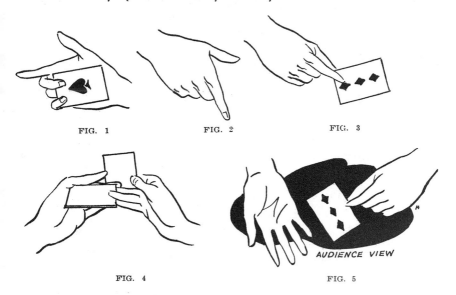

FIG. 1   FIG. 2   FIG. 3

FIG. 4   FIG. 5

In the course of this snap production both hands can be shown empty in succession in the following manner. Take hold of the outer top corner of the card just produced by the right thumb and forefinger, slide these digits along the upper edge of the card to the middle and turn it to a vertical position, Fig. 4, stretch out three fingers of the right hand, put the packet of cards in the left thumb crotch and grip them there, at the same moment making a turn to the right. Keep the left forefinger on the face of the visible card and extend the other three fingers below, the cards will then be concealed by the left fingers of the visible card. Remove the right hand and show it empty. Fig. 5.

Take hold of the visible card at the middle of the side with the tips of the thumb and forefinger as before and, in turning to the left, grip the end of the packet between the top joints of the last three fingers and swing them back to their first position against the right palm. Show the left hand empty, take the visible card from the right hand and continue with the production.

This change over of the packet from the right hand to the left, and vice versa, will be found to present no difficulty but it should not be repeated too often. Do it after the second or third card has been produced and then once more prior to the production of the last card.

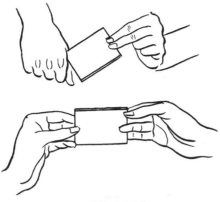

FIG. 6 and 7

In order to pass from the squeeze production to the snap production, proceed as follows: Bring the left hand over the packet of cards squeezed out of the right hand and take it by the middle of the upper end between the tips of the thumb and first two fingers, Fig. 6. Turn slightly towards the right and show the right hand empty.

Next take the free end of the pack between the tips of the right thumb and fingers, at the same time slipping the top joint of the third finger behind the packet, Fig. 7. Turn towards the left and remove the left hand which carries away the face card at the tips of the thumb and fingers at the same time, close the three fingers of the right hand thus swinging the remaining cards of the packet back against the right palm. The right forefinger remaining extended and pointing to the card in the left hand. The hands should be at about the level of the waist.

Both hands have thus been shown empty and the cards are in position for the snap production.

More Card Manipulations

SERIES 3

Illustrations by Nelson Hahne

More Card Manipulations No. 3

CONTENTS

More Card Manipulations No. 3

THE FACED DECK — THE SECRET TURN OVER

The principle of the faced deck and the secret turn over is one of the oldest in card conjuring. The first mention of it that I have found is in Decremps, Testament de Jerome Sharpe, (1793), and his explanation reads as follows:—"Hold the cards at the end of the left hand, Fig. 1, so that by closing the hand, they can be turned over, top to bottom, and they will be found, after the hand is opened, anew, as in Fig. 2. (They will not appear to have been turned over, because they show a white side above and below.)" French playing cards of the period had plain white backs, the patterned backs being a later developement.

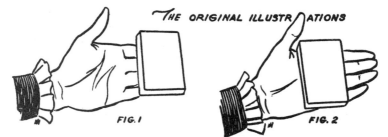

THE ORIGINAL ILLUSTRATIONS

FIG. 1   FIG. 2

In Modern Magic (1876) Professor Hoffman described a later method. He says: "Take the pack flat in the left hand, the fingers clipping it rather tightly, but without the aid of the thumb. Press the thumb underneath, and with the ball of the thumb press the pack smartly upwards (see Fig. 3), when it will describe a semi-revolution on its longer axis, the lower face of the pack being thereby brought uppermost."

FIG. 3

A still later method, and the one in popular use at the present time is to hold the pack in the left hand as for dealing, drop the hand to the side and, at the same time, turn it over bringing its back uppermost. When the hand is then raised, the pack has been turned over, the original lower half being uppermost. Figs. 4 and 5.

The drawback to all three methods is that the necessary movement of the pack has to be covered by a quick and unnatural movement of the hand and arm, or by very strong misdirection, such as the accidental dropping of a card to the floor, the sleight being executed under cover of the action of picking up the card. In the following method these drawbacks are eliminated and the sleight becomes a simple and natural move.

The halves of the deck having been brought face to face secretly, when it becomes necessary to turn the deck over to bring the cards of the lower portion uppermost, proceed as follows:—Hold the deck in the right hand between the thumb, at the lower left corner, and the top joint of the third finger, at the upper right corner. Fig. 6. Press all four fingers close together, so that the pack is practically hidden by the back of the hand.

FIG. 4   FIG. 5   FIG. 6

Bring the hands together in the act of placing the pack in the left hand and, in doing so, press the tip of the right first finger on the upper left corner. This downward pressure will cause the pack to pivot on the two diagonally opposite corners which are held by the thumb and forefinger and the required half turn is made imperceptible as the pack is placed quite naturally in the left hand. The right hand then moves away, or continues the deal, according to the requirements of the trick in hand.

The principle of the faced deck has been neglected by modern magicians. One of the few tricks in which it is used is the Four Ace Trick. Every now and then someone bobs up in print with this **new** method of working the trick by means of the faced deck, unconscious of the fact that this was the original method which is fully explained in

Nouvelle Magie Blanche Devoilee, published in Paris in 1853. (See page 172, Encyclopedia of Card Tricks). It may well be noted here that the trick of the red and black aces changing places from the top and bottom of the pack to the middle and vice versa, is claimed by the author of this book, J. N. Ponsin, as his original invention.

THE GAMBLER'S TABLE CHANGE

By means of this ingenious sleight a card, which has been shown and openly dropped face down on the table, is imperceptibly changed to another card. At first sight the sleight may appear to be a difficult one, but a little practice will show it to be comparatively easy. That it is practicable is proved by the fact that gamblers use it to change their hole card in stud poker under the eyes of their opponents.

To execute the sleight proceed as follows:

1. Show a card, face outwards, holding it by the sides between the right thumb and middle finger, the forefinger resting on the middle of the back. By pulling upwards with the thumb and finger and pressing downwards with the forefinger, crimp the card slightly lengthwise in laying it on the table, face down, to your right. Fig. 1.

2. Pick up the pack with your right hand and put it in your left hand, at the same time palming the top card in the right hand by the one hand top palm—(Card Manipulations No. 1, page 2).

3. Remark casually: "By the way, what was the card I showed you?" Move the right hand to the left side of the table card, slide the outer side of the palmed card under it,—the crimp making this insertion easy,—keep the hand flat and push the palmed card under the table card, at the same time resting the little finger side of the hand on the table. Turn the thumb side of the hand upwards, pivoting on the little finger side, and with the tip of the thumb bend up the side of the original table card which is now above the other card. Bend your head down to look at it and call its name. Fig. 2.

4. Turn the hand down as if to press the card flat on the table again, but hold the exchanged card by pressing the tip of the little finger on its outer right hand corner while the base of the thumb presses against the card's inner left corner, Fig. 3. By means of this method the hand can be pressed down on the table quite flat and still retain the card, a position which apparently negatives all possibility of palming.

5. Take the pack in the right hand, adding the palmed card to it in the action.

This sleight is not only useful as a means of getting out of a difficulty caused by the accidental production of a wrong card, but also for getting possession of a card which it is necessary to dispose of in some special way, or again for changing a chosen card into a prominent person's photograph on some special occasion and so on.

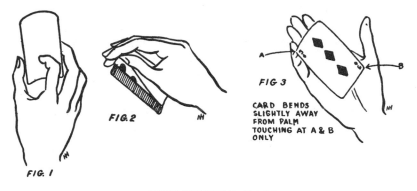

FIG 3

CARD BENDS
SLIGHTLY AWAY
FROM PALM
TOUCHING AT A & B
ONLY

FIG.2

FIG. I

THE SPREAD PASS

This pass has been familiar to me for a long time but so far as I know it has never appeared in print and I do not know who devised it. The sleight calls for the return of a selected card to the pack as the cards are spread between the hands. It is covered by the natural movement of closing the spread and is indetectible.

To execute the sleight proceed as follows:

1. Spread the cards for the choice of one keeping the hands rather close together, the tips of the little fingers touching under the spread.

2. Have the chosen card replaced about the middle of the spread. Under cover of the cards above it and you begin to close the spread by bringing the right hand towards the left hand, slip the tips of the left first and fourth fingers underneath the bottom card of the deck and the tips of the left second and third fingers on top of the chosen card. Press these fingers inwards, squaring this lower packet, on top of which lies the chosen card, against the base of the left thumb. Fig 1.

3. Continue the action of closing the spread with the right hand, the cards of the upper section resting on the lower part of the right forefinger. Straighten out all the fingers of the right hand and turn the hand to a vertical position, thus lifting the right hand side

of this packet as the left hand side strikes against the fork of the left thumb, squaring the packet.

4. At the same moment extend the left fingers, lifting and turning the lower packet outwards so that it strikes against the inside of the right hand. Fig. 2.

5. As the edges of the two packets clear one another, let the top packet fall from the fork of the left thumb into that hand and close the lower packet on it with the right hand, at once moving the right thumb and fingers along the ends of the deck as if merely squaring the cards.

The action should be accompanied by a slight swing of the hands towards the left so that the transposition of the packets is covered by the back of the right hand. Smoothness and not rapidity should be aimed at.

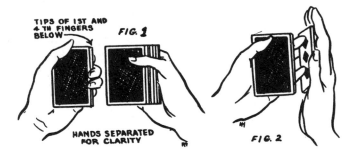

TIPS OF 1ST AND 4 TH FINGERS BELOW

FIG. 1

HANDS SEPARATED FOR CLARITY

FIG. 2

THE THUMB SLIDE

This method of controlling a card after its return to the pack was, I believe, first described by Professor Hoffman many years ago in a foot note in Selbit's Magazine, "The Wizard." He credited it to Hartz, "the Devil of a Hat man." The sleight does not appear to have found its way into any of the textbooks or to have come into general use, yet, with the additional move described below it is well worth attention.

A card having been drawn, hold the pack in the left hand, Fig. 1, divide it into two parts by taking about one-third of the pack with the right hand between the top joints of the second and third fingers at the outer end and the top joint of the thumb at the inner end, Fig. 2. Note that the tip of the thumb protrudes below the packet.

Have the chosen card replaced on the cards in the left hand, which you hold firmly between the fingers and the thumb which lies along the left side of the packet, thus allowing the replaced card to lie loosely on the others. Bring the right hand packet over the left hand packet and a little in front of it, so that the tip of the thumb strikes the back of the loose card at about the middle of its back. Fig. 3. Bring the right hand back towards the body and rapidly ex-

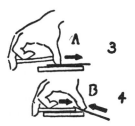

tend the thumb sliding the card inwards. As soon as the card clears the inner end of the right hand packet, press down on it with the tip of the thumb, tilting the front end of the card upwards, Fig. 4. At once move the thumb forwards, bringing the card to the top of the pack as the two packets are made to coalesce.

Continue the forward movement of the thumb making the card it controls slightly overlap the pack at the outer end, Fig. 5. Press the tips of the right fingers on the protruding outer end of the card,

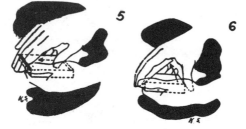

tilting it upwards into the right hand which palms it, Fig. 6.   Run the
fingers and thumb of the right hand along the ends of the pack squaring
it and then hold the pack in that hand by tne left corners,
showing as much of it as possible.

The action of the right thumb is covered by the fingers which
are held close together.   The whole movement can be executed so
rapidly and smoothly that it is impossible for the onlooker to imagine
that the card has been brought to the top and palmed off.

NEW METHOD OF PICKING UP AN ARRANGED DECK
After It Has Been Spread On The Table And A
Card Has Been Withdrawn From It

When a set-up deck has been spread on the table and a spectator
has drawn a card from the line, the usual method of picking
up the cards is this:—The left hand half of the spread is taken first,
starting from the space left in the row by the removal of the selected
card and the remaining cards are picked up by sliding this packet
under the card at the right hand end of the row, gathering them by
a sweep of the right hand towards the left.   Thus the card that was
above the selected card becomes the bottom card of the deck and a
glimpse of it reveals the name of the chosen card.   This is the method
explained by Robert-Houdin on page 228 of his Secrets of Conjuring
and Magic and it has remained in vogue all these years.

The picking up of the cards from the middle of the row is unnatural,
even when done casually and the action is liable to arouse
suspicion in the minds of the spectators, and is a sure give-away to
those who know the principle of the prearranged deck.   To avoid
this, operate as follows:

The spread is made from right to left.   After a card has been
removed, place your right hand at the right end of the row, the left

hand at the other end. Insert the right fingers under the last card and the right thumb over it, Fig. 1. Move the right hand towards the left, gathering the cards, drop the tip of the thumb on the back of the card that was below the one removed, Fig. 2, and continue the movement. The cards above the thumb tip will slide together loosely into the left hand between the left thumb and fingers and the right hand puts the cards it holds on top of them.

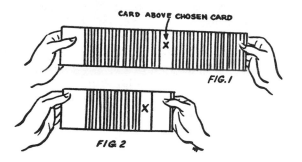

The swing of the hands towards the left covers the pass completely for the left hand moves away a little, as it receives the upper packet, and the right hand puts its cards on top in the natural action of squaring the cards. The whole action is easy and the suspicious movement of gathering the cards in two sections is done away with.

AN EASY FORCE

Place the card to be forced tenth from the top. This can be done by having the card on the top of the pack and running nine cards on it in the course of an overhand shuffle. Then make a false shuffle and several false cuts, leaving the top section of the pack undisturbed.

Ask a spectator to name a number between one and ten. We will suppose that eight is named. At once begin dealing the cards but, when you have put down two cards, that is to say, the difference between eight and ten, stop and say to the spectator: "It will be better if you take the cards and make the count yourself so that you will be satisfied that there is no trickery." Casually drop the remaining cards on the two cards just dealt and push the pack towards him.

In the unlikely event of four or a smaller number being named, you say: "That is rather small so I will ask for another number from someone else, say between one and five, so that there can be no possible suspicion of collusion in the matter."

A second number having been called, add the two together and proceed as explained above.

REVERSING THE BOTTOM CARD — TWO METHODS

WORKING—Invite a spectator to shuffle the pack, take it back and shuffle it yourself. It is necessary now to bring the cards into a face-up position with the former top card (now the lowermost) secretly reversed after it has been sighted. There are many ways of doing this. For example, you can spread the cards face up to show they have been mixed thoroughly, glimpse the upper index of the top card which lies against the left palm and, as you close the spread with a slight swing of the hands towards the left, catch the left side of this card against the roots of the left fingers, close these fingers, pressing them against the back of the card, thus imperceptibly turning it face down under cover of the others.

To learn this simple move, hold your left hand palm upwards and place one card face up on the fingers so that its left side is along the roots of the fingers. Bend the fingers upwards against the right side of the card turning it face down onto the palm. Then do the same thing under cover of closing the spread of face-up cards.

Second Method: Having sighted the bottom card as you take the pack back, make an overhand shuffle bringing this card to the top, then repeat the shuffle sending it to the bottom again. Hold

Fig. 1

the pack face down in your left hand, as for dealing, grasp it between the right fingers at the outer end and the thumb at the inner end, the tip of the forefinger resting on the middle of the top card. Bend the ends of the card upwards, let the inner end of the bottom card slip free from the thumb and push the remainder of the pack forward about an inch over the left forefinger, Fig. 1. Seize the outer end of the pack between the right thumb above and the fingers below, and turn it over lengthwise towards your body onto the bottom card which remains face down. A slight upward movement of the hands provides perfect cover and the action is a natural one.

THE CARLYLE FALSE COUNT

This method of false counting is valuable for several reasons. It is made in the natural way of taking cards one by one from the left hand with the right, the cards being held as for dealing them, and there is no visible difference in the action when the cards are counted as fewer, or more, than they really are.

We will suppose, for example, that the packet to be counted consists of ten cards. Hold it in the left hand, the right outer corner resting against the top joint of the 1st finger which presses the opposite diagonal corner, the left inner corner, of the packet against the palm below the base of the thumb. The left outer corner rests against the second joint of the forefinger and the second and third lightly grip the side of the cards and the little finger is free at the right side of the packet, taking no part in the action. Fig. 1.

NOTE: The first finger should be at the right upper corner pressing cards into the base of the thumb. Second and third fingers along side of cards.

I. To Count a Number of Cards Showing Less Than There Are.

Let us suppose that you wish to count the packet of ten cards as six only. Hold the packet exactly as described above. With the left thumb push off the top card and, as the hands come together, take it between the top joints of the right thumb and forefinger, carrying it away as you count "One." Bring the hands together again, push off the second card with the left thumb and take it between the top joints of the right first and second fingers, immediately afterwards withdrawing the first finger from between the two cards and placing it below them, counting "Two." This action of the forefinger is important and must be repeated with each card counted off.

Continue the count in exactly the same way up to and including the fifth card. Five cards then remain in the left hand, perfectly squared thanks to the manner in which the packet is held. Take these five cards as one only, exactly the same way as the single cards were taken except that the left thumb merely moves forward over the back of the packet and back again without moving the top card. Count "Six."

Throw down one card and repeat the count exactly as before, this time taking the packet of four cards at the count of "Six." Throw down another card and repeat the count taking the packet of three as one card and continue in the same way until six cards only are left.

When the method of holding the packet is understood there is not the least difficulty in the action, but this hold must be rigidly adhered to throughout. The cards in the left hand must not be spread in the least degree when the top card is pushed forward by the left thumb.

II. To Count a Number of Cards as More Than They Really Are.

We will suppose that you have a packet of ten cards and that you wish to count them as eleven. In this case the illusion depends upon the left thumb smartly pulling back, square with the packet, the card that it pushes forward as if to be taken by the right hand. Hold the packet exactly as described for the first method. Push the top card off with the left thumb, then pull it back rapidly by the reverse action of the thumb to its first position square with the rest of the packet. Practice this movement until you can do it very rapidly without spreading the cards below it, a matter of a few minutes only.

Now to make the false count, begin in the same way as in the first method. At, we will say, the sixth card, push it forward with the left thumb as usual, make the motion of taking it between the right first and second fingers, separating the second finger to receive it, and at the same moment with the left thumb pull it back smartly onto the packet in the left hand. Move the right first finger in exactly the same way as when a card is really taken and continue the count as before, thus making it appear that there are eleven cards. It is important that the tempo of the count remain the same throughout.

Smoothly done the illusion is perfect. The false count can be repeated as many times as may be necessary for the trick in hand. Mr. Carlyle makes a special use of it for an amusing interlude between other tricks. He takes, let us say, eleven cards from the pack and announces a trick in which he will use just eight cards. He counts the cards and finds that there are nine. Apologizing for the mistake, he throws down one card. "Now for the trick," he says, "we have eight cards." He counts them and again he has nine. Rather bewildered he discards another one and again he counts the cards. This time he really has nine cards so it is a straight count. Nine cards again. Angered, he throws down another card and once more counts nine cards by making one false count. Thoroughly disgusted and unable to understand what is the matter, he hands the eight cards to a spectator asking him to count them. The person does so and finds that there are exactly eight cards.

"Well, that's fine," says Carlyle. "NOW I'll be able to do the trick. Watch just eight cards," and again he counts them. There are nine. "You must have made a mistake," he says and he throws down a card. "Now for it." He makes another count and still finds nine cards. He throws down another card and counts once more, still there are nine. In despair he throws all the cards down, gives the trick up as a bad job and goes on to something else.

Those who are familiar with the old "Six Card Repeat" routine will find this Carlyle method of false counting invaluable.

THE MILLER CARD CASE

So far in this series I have avoided descriptions of any apparatus or fakes but I feel that an exception should be made in favor of this ingenious card case.

The case is an ordinary flap card case such as is used for Bicycle cards and it is prepared in such a way that any number of cards, up to about eight, can be added to the pack imperceptibly.

To make it two cases are necessary. From one cut off the face, opposite to the flap, making the cut along the 5/16 white margin on the sides and bottom. Discard the face side. Take the remaining half (original back of case) Fig. 1, cut off the flap and fit it over the other case on the flap side. Glue the two sides and the end of this cover to the case so that its edges coincide with the top of the white margin along the lower side. A pocket is thus made on the flap side of the case, Fig. 2, which will hold six or eight cards and these can be allowed to slide out at will. When the flap is opened and pressed back, the pocket is hidden completely and when the case is viewed from the closed end the preparation is imperceptible.

When the pocket is loaded and a pack is inside the case, you have only to pull out the flap, bend it back over the pocket and the pack can be removed under the eyes of a spectator. You can allow him to see plainly that the case is empty. When the flap is closed and the other end is turned towards him, the pocket cannot be detected.

Apart from its general utility for loading cards onto a shuffled deck, it can be used for an effective trick, the passing of several selected cards into the case while the pack is held by a spectator. The trick may be called "The Homing Cards."

Load the pocket beforehand with duplicates of the cards to be forced. To do the trick: Open the flap, bend it back, shake out the cards and call attention to the fact that the case is empty. Turn it, close the flap and lay it down with the flap end away from the spectators.

Force the cards, three we will say, have them replaced, bring them to the top or bottom, palm them in the right or left hand as preferred, and hand the pack to a spectator. Order the three cards to pass back to the empty case and have the pack examined to prove that they have vanished. Show your hands empty, take the case, open the flap and let the hidden cards slide from the pocket into the left hand, which hides the fact that they come from behind the flap, the back of the left hand being towards the spectators.

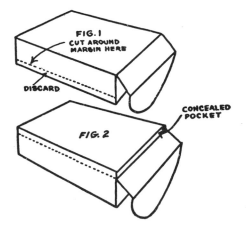

THE COTTONE SPIDER-GRIP FALSE CUT

To execute this entirely new and deceptive false cut, it is necessary to pay particular attention to the mechanics of the movement. Hold the deck face down in the right hand between the second and third fingers at the outer end and the thumb at the inner end, the first and fourth fingers grip the sides of the deck about an inch from the corners of the outer end, Fig. 1. Grip the inner end

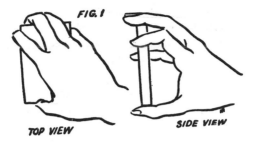

FIG. 1

TOP VIEW   **SIDE VIEW**

of the pack from below with the left hand between the thumb on one side and the second and third finger tips on the other. The tips of the right thumb and fingers must extend about half an inch below the deck, Fig. 2. This is the correct position of the hands and the cards

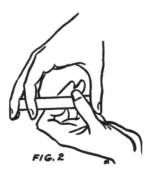

FIG. 2

but before making the false cut, drop the outer end of the pack a little downwards.

To make the false cut: Release the grip of the right thumb and with it raise the inner end of the top card very slightly. With the right first and little fingers pressing against the sides of the deck, pull forward this top card together with the lower half of the deck. Fig. 3. As the packets clear one another press the top card onto the

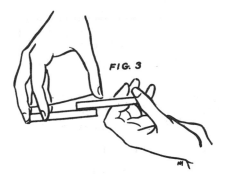

FIG. 3

lower half of the deck with the right thumb tip and again grip the inner end of the packet with the thumb. Drop this packet on the table or on a spectator's hand. Grip the packet remaining in the left hand with the right thumb and fingers at the ends and drop it on top of the original lower packet.

This false cut has displaced the top card, sending it to the middle of the deck but leaving the rest of the cards in their original order.

The right second and third fingers must be kept apart and the corners of the pack remain in full view. This enables the spectator to see the top card throughout and thus completes the illusion.

TRICKS USING THE SPIDER-GRIP FALSE CUT

1. A Stubborn Card

Having placed the Joker secretly third from the top, make a triple lift and show it as being the top card. Replace the three cards as one and execute the Spider-grip cut. Make a double lift and show the Joker still on the top. Replace the two cards as one and do the Hindu shuffle bringing the two cards again to the top. Double lift again and show the Joker. Replace the two cards as one and again make the Spider-grip cut. Show the Joker still on the top.

2. Gambler's Sense of Touch

Control a selected card, bringing it to the bottom. Make the Spider-grip false cut, pulling out the bottom half of the pack with the top card. Have the chosen card named and turn the right hand packet face upwards, proving that you have cut at the very card.

3. The Penetrating Eye

Memorize the three top cards and make a false shuffle keeping them on the top. Execute the Spider-grip cut with one-third of the deck, taking the top card, and put the packet on the table. Repeat the sleight with half the remaining cards and the original second card. Place this packet beside the first and put the remaining packet beside it. Now call the names of the three top cards.

By memorizing the six top cards you can repeat the trick at once with very good effect. You have merely to place the original top packet on the other two and repeat the false cuts.

4. The Four Aces Are Tops

Get the four Aces secretly to the top of the pack and false shuffle leaving them there. Execute the Spider-grip cuts making four heaps on the table. Turn the top card face upwards, showing an ace each time. An excellent way to begin a "Four Ace Trick."

5. Poker Heaps

Secretly arrange a pat poker hand on the top of the deck. Begin by making a false shuffle retaining the five cards on the top. By means of the Spider-grip false cut divide the pack into five heaps. Turn the top card of each heap face upwards and show that they make a regular poker hand.

6. Digging For Diamonds

Place the thirteen Diamonds on the bottom of the pack with one indifferent card on them; make this arrangement secretly.

Show the pack face up in the left hand, the indifferent card showing on its face. Execute the Spider-grip cut and drop the packet in the right hand on the table. Call attention to the Diamond on the face of the left hand packet. Repeat the movements and again show a Diamond on the face of the left hand packet. Continue the cuts, showing a Diamond each time until Diamonds only remain in your left hand. Place this packet, face up or face down, on the table and invite a spectator to cut. He also gets a Diamond. Before he has time to investigate, take the cut from him, reassemble the pack and shuffle, before proceeding to another trick.

The preceding effects afford excellent examples of the great usefulness of this new sleight which will undoubtedly become an indispensable weapon in the armory of the up-to-date card worker.

TRICKS

PICKING A POCKET

EFFECT—A card having been freely chosen and replaced, the pack is put into a spectator's outside coat pocket. The magician pulls the card through the lining of the pocket.

WORKING—Any deck can be used. Have it freely shuffled and allow a spectator to select a card, note what it is and return it to the pack. Control it by the pass, the Hindu shuffle or your own pet pass substitute, bringing it to the top, and palm the card in your right hand.

Place the pack in the left outside coat pocket of the spectator's coat with your left hand, at the same time grasping the lower edge of the coat, just below the pocket, with the right hand and introducing the card underneath. Push it upwards and hold it for the moment between the tips of the right first and second fingers under the coat and the thumb on the outside. Now grasp the front edge of the coat with the left hand and hold the card with the tips of the fingers underneath and the thumb on the outside.

Release the right hand and, showing it empty by your gestures, say that you will pull the chosen card right through the lining of the coat. Make a pretense of plucking at the bottom of the pocket under the cloth. Grip the end of the card with the tips of the right second and third fingers, remove the left hand, casually showing it empty. Then with it take hold of a part of the cloth outside the bottom of the pocket and pull it outwards as if trying to tear it away from the lining inside.

Finally have the card named and pull it away from under the coat with the right hand. Let the spectator remove the pack from his pocket which, of course, is intact.

MARRIED COUPLES AND BACHELORS

This amusing and effective trick requires the use of two double faced cards. I have up to the present, in this series, avoided the use of prepared cards, however, an exception should be made in the case of double faced cards since they can be introduced into a borrowed deck for a special effect and secretly abstracted afterwards. Their use in this manner opens up an intriguing field to the card worker; the fact that the deck in use is a borrowed one makes the effects a hundred per cent more effective than when one's own cards are used.

The two cards required are the same, they show a Jack of Clubs on one side and a Queen of Diamonds on the other. The only other articles necessary are two rectangles of cardboard, about seven inches by five or, in place of these, two newspapers can be folded to about the same dimensions and they will serve the purpose equally well. To prepare for the trick you have merely to place the two prepared cards in your left trousers pocket, one with the Jack of Clubs face outwards, the other with the Queen of Diamonds facing the same way, and place the two newspapers on your table.

WORKING AND PRESENTATION—Begin by folding the two papers to the required size and lay them on your table, one on each side. Borrow a pack of cards, and note here, that it is advisable to have planted a pack with someone in the audience in case one should not be forthcoming. This is permissible seeing that the pack is not prepared in any way. In the meantime, you have seized a favorable opportunity to palm the two faked cards in your left hand. Receive the pack in your right hand and add the two palmed cards to it in laying the pack face upwards on your left palm. Spread about half the cards face up with your right hand, take them off and show them to the spectators as you ask the owner of the pack if he is sure the cards are just regular cards. Replace these cards underneath those in your left hand, bringing the two prepared cards to the middle so that you can handle the pack quite freely.

Take your position behind the table and say: "I propose to illustrate a little drama in which six characters will take part. Two married couples and two bachelors." Run over the faces of the cards, take out the two prepared cards and lay them face up on the table as the Jack of Clubs and the Queen of Diamonds, being careful not to expose the double faces in so doing. Next search for and take out the King and Queen of Hearts, the King of Diamonds and the Jack of Spades and in laying these cards face up on the table carelessly allow the backs to be seen. Further in removing these last four cards you have slipped the regular Queen of Diamonds and the Jack of Clubs secretly to the top of the pack.

Lay the pack aside and call attention to the fact that you use six cards only from the borrowed deck. Arrange the cards, all faces upwards, on the table which should be covered with a cloth to facilitate the picking up of the cards, as shown in Fig. 1.

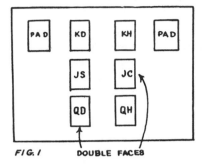

FIG. 1   DOUBLE FACES

"Now" you continue, "I ask you to imagine that the scene is a drawing room in which the two married couples, the King and Queen of Hearts and the King and Queen of Diamonds, meet the two gay young bachelors, the Jack of Spades and the Jack of Clubs."

As you name each card pick it up to show it plainly and the manner in which you take the cards for this purpose is important. Take each one in turn with the tips of the first three fingers at the end nearest to you, the tip of the middle finger on the face of the card, the tips of the first and third fingers underneath, Fig. 2. Lift each

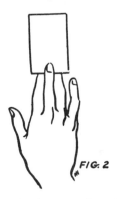

FIG. 2

card from the back letting the front end rest on the table so that the face is directly towards the spectators.

"These two papers will represent a little retiring room on the right and a cozy boudoir on the left." Lift them, showing them and replace them. "After the usual greetings, remarks about the weather and so on, the two husbands excuse themselves and go to the billiard room to enjoy a smoke and to talk over matters of business."

Picking up the Kings of Hearts and Diamonds, showing them, as describe above, at the finger tips, and lay them aside, face down, on the table.

"When they had gone the Jack of Spades,—note the come hither look in his eye,—went into the little room on the left and the Queen of Diamonds at once joined him."

Lift the paper on your left with your left hand by taking hold of the side nearest to you and raising it, letting the front edge remain touching the table. Pick up the Jack of Spades with the tips of the fingers of the right hand, as explained, and place it behind the paper face upwards, letting the paper fall on it. Pick up the Queen of Diamonds, always in the same way, show it, lift the rear side of the paper on the left with the left hand as before and lay the Queen on the Jack of Spades, turning it over with the fingers and being careful not to turn the hand and wrist in the action.

In the meantime the Queen of Hearts strolled into the boudoir on the right and, very naturally, the Jack of Clubs followed her.

Raise the right-hand pad with the left hand, the Queen of Hearts with the right fingers, place the card behind the pad, face upwards and let the pad fall on it. Pick up the Jack of Clubs in the same way, raise the rear side of the pad and place the Jack under it, turning the card in the same way as you did the Queen of Diamonds, and let the pad fall over both cards.

"In the midst of these intriguing flirtations, the two husbands returned to the drawingroom. The demon of Jealousy is at work and all is set for a lively scene. However, Cupid was on the alert and, on going to the little room on the left, the two kings found the gay young bachelors quietly discussing the merits of their cars." Lift the pad and reveal the two Jacks face upwards, lift them by the ends nearest you with the finger tips and show them, then lay them down, faces upwards, with the pad beside them. "And in the boudoir they see the two Queens busily discussing the latest fashions." Lift the right hand pad, raise the Queens with the tips of the right fingers, showing them, then lay them face up on the table beside the pad.

"Perfectly reassured, the two husbands, their jealous suspicions removed, rejoin their friends in the smoking room." Put them aside as before. Take the two Jacks by the ends nearest to you, show them as before, raise the rear end of the left pad with the left hand, put the cards behind it, turning them as explained, and let the pad fall on them; do the same with the two Queens on the right.

"After waiting prudently for several minutes to make sure that the husbands had gone . . . . . . the inevitable, I might say the biologically inevitable, happens. In the little room here (lift the pad) the Jack of Spades is embracing the Queen of Diamonds (show them and in the boudoir (lift the pad) the Queen of Hearts is in the loving arms of the ardent Jack of Clubs."

After having shown the face of the Jack of Spades, replace the card face down on the Queen of Diamonds, take both cards with the tips of the fingers as usual, raise the rear edge of the pad, put the cards behind it, turning them as before, and drop the pad on them. In the same way show the face of the Queen of Hearts, replace the card face down on the Jack of Clubs and secretly turn the two cards, masking the action with the pad as usual.

"In due course the husbands return from their soothing session with the tranquil weed, little suspecting what was going on in their absence. This suspense is terrible, isn't it? However, once more they find the two innocent young men in the little room on the left (lift the pad and display the two Jacks face up) and in the boudoir the two ladies still chatting amicably (lift the right pad and show the faces of the two Queens.) So they were quite satisfied . . . . . and everybody was happy."

Gather the six cards face up with the two prepared cards at the bottom of the packet. Place the pack face up on the packet, then lift the whole pack, square the cards and palm off the two prepared cards in the left hand. Pocket these as you return the pack to its owner. Any examination of the pack will heighten the mystery.

It is essential that the cards be held always at the finger tips as described so that the necessary turns can be made without the slightest movement of the hand or wrist.

A similar effect, but one presented without any covers, was created by Gerald L. Kaufman in 1935 and has been advertised and sold, with his permission, by Al. Baker, under the title "The King Can Do No Wrong." The rather risque patter, however, makes this trick unsuitable for this series.

SPRINGING THE TRAP

EFFECT—A newspaper is spread on a table and on it two glasses are placed. On these is laid a metal plate in the middle of which there is a rectangular hole just large enough to allow for the passage of a pack of cards. A spectator is invited to choose a card freely, replace it and shuffle the cards himself. The pack is then placed in the hole in the plate and it is supported in that position by one card placed underneath it as in Fig. 1.

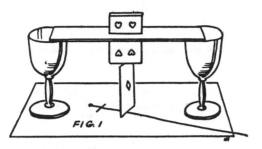

FIG. 1

The spectator is requested to name his card and to blow towards the pack; at once all the cards fall, with the exception of the one he chose, which remains in the hole in the plate.

WORKING—The glasses are unprepared and the metal plate is quite plain but the hole in it is of such size that the narrow ends of a stripper deck will pass through while the wide ends will not. The newspaper is a full sheet doubled and, at about the middle of the upper half, a small slit is cut. Fasten a small bead to a black thread and pass the bead through the slit between the two thicknesses of the paper. To the other end of the thread affix a small pellet of wax and adjust the length of the thread so that it reaches a little beyond the edge of the paper. The arrangement is shown in the figure.

Lay the newspaper on the table, the side with the slit upper-most and place the two glasses in position. Invite a spectator to choose a card freely from a stripper deck, see that it is replaced reversed and allow him to shuffle the cards. Take the deck back, remove one card and pass the pack upwards through the hole in the metal plate. Place the single card crosswise under the lower end of the deck to support it, as shown in the figure.

Instruct the spectator to name his card and to blow hard towards the pack at the word three. Stand at the right side of your table, pick up your wand and the wax pellet. Tap the wand on the table, counting one, two, three. At the third tap jerk the wand back a little towards your body, pulling the bead through the slit and thus dislodging the supporting card. All the cards except the reversed chosen card fall through the hole in the plate to the table and it remains alone facing the spectators.

THE TWO PILE MYSTERY

Card tricks can be divided into four classes. There are a few which are suitable for stage presentation, a goodly number can be presented effectively before small audiences, a huge number are suitable for the drawing room and there are many which, to obtain their full effect, must be done when seated at a table with a few friends. This trick belongs to the last category. It is one of the best of its class.

EFFECT—Two cards, selected while the magician's back is turned, are found in a mysterious manner. No questions are asked of the drawers.

WORKING—Spectators A and B agree privately on a small number. Hand the pack, any pack can be used, to A to shuffle. Then instruct him to deal cards to the number agreed upon in a pile face downwards, while you turn your back. This done, he hands the remainder of the deck to B to shuffle, and B in his turn deals a face down pile of the same number of cards. Each of them then notes the bottom card of his pile and remembers it.

Next A places his pile on top of the remaining cards, squares the deck carefully, while B covers his pile with his hands so that you cannot possibly make any estimate of the number of cards it contains. You then turn and take the cards from A. Addressing him you say that you will try to discover the number agreed upon between them by watching his face as you deal the cards and warn him that, most likely, he will be unable to avoid giving some indication by a change of expression when you reach the number. Make a false shuffle and several blind cuts, retaining about a dozen cards on the top intact. Deal nine cards deliberately face down, while gazing steadfastly at A, apparently without result. Acknowledge that you have failed to get the number and congratulate A on having a good poker face. Say that you will have to discover his card by unconscious cerebration or any other high-faulting nonsense you care to use. The fact is that this is purely a bluff to enable you to reverse the top nine cards in an unsuspicious way, the success of the trick depending on this reversal.

Replace the nine cards on top of the pack in their present order, but before doing so tap the packet on the table to square it, note and remember the bottom card which will be your key card. False shuffle once more, keeping the top cards intact.

Turn away and instuct B to place his packet on top of the pack, and square the cards carefully. Make the excuse that you will try to find his card by a different method to avoid the risk of making two failures in succession. The packet having been replaced, turn, take the pack and false shuffle again. A's card will now be the tenth card from the top of the deck. Turn the pack face upwards, spread the upper half of the pack and invite A to make a free choice of any spot card. We will suppose that he chooses a six spot. Mentally deduct six from ten, thumb count four cards from the top of the pack which is now against your left palm, the pack being still face upwards, and palm them in your left hand. Divert attention from your hands by asking A to show his six spot to everyone and then to lay it face up on the table.

Turn the pack face down in your left hand and hold it in position for dealing, the palmed cards will be hidden and the appearance of the left hand will be quite natural. Deal five cards face down in a row, overlapping each other slightly so that later you can count to any one of them at a glance. Fig. 1. Put the sixth card aside face down and ask A to name his card. As he does so, turn the pack face up lengthwise, making a remark about not being sure that A's subconscious self has impelled him to the right card. Fan the top cards, those nearest the left palm, and note at what number the key card lies. Suppose it is the third card, add one to it and you have the number at which B's card lay before you palmed the four cards, that is to say it was the fourth card and four is also the number that A and B originally decided upon.

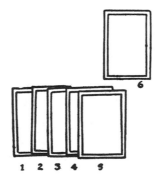

Fig. 1

Add the palmed cards to the pack and turn it face down. Since you know the position of B's card it is an easy matter to leave it at the top in shuffling, then make a double lift showing an indifferent card as B's card. B, of course says it is a wrong card, so you turn the cards face down, take the top card and put it face down be side A's. Have both A and B name their cards and turn the two cards face up.

Finally, after pointing out that you can have no possible clue to the number of cards each spectator counted off originally, spread the whole pack face up and ask both spectators to hold your right wrist. Pass your left hand over the line of cards and after the usual tremors and hesitation drop your forefinger on a card whose spots equal the number you have already arrived at, in this case, four.

The onlookers can have no conception as to how you were able to find the cards or the number secretly agreed upon; the whole thing is incomprehensible to them and very effective.

Synopsis

A and B secretly agree on small number between 1 and 10.
Turn away; A shuffles, then deals face down to number.
B shuffles, deals to same number. Each note bottom cards.
A places packet on pack, squares cards; B hides his packet.
Turn, take pack; deal nine cards reversing order.
Replace on pack, noting bottom card, Key card.
Turn away; B places packet on pack, squares cards.
False shuffle. A's card now tenth from top of pack.
Turn pack face up, A draws any spot card, a six, for example.
Deduct 6 from 10, 4; bottom palm four cards in left hand.
Turn pack face down, deal 5 cards overlapping; sixth put aside.
Spread cards, note position of key card from top, say fourth.
Add 1 to 4, 5.

B's card was fifth before palming four cards.
It is, therefore the first card dealt on the table.
Five is the number secretly agreed upon by A and B.

MENE, TEKEL, UPHARSIN — (The Thirty Cards)
ALPHA TO OMEGA

For many generations, the trick of passing several cards from one counted packet to another has been a favorite with both magicians and audiences. The first recorded form of the trick that I have been able to trace is that written by J. N. Posin in his Nouvelle

Magie Blanche Devoilee, published in Paris in 1853. Even in its early form the trick is a good one, as will be seen by the following translation of Ponsin's explanation of it. This translation is a literal one and the reader will get a good idea of Ponsin's style from it. He called the trick—

THE MULTIPLICATION OF CARDS WHILE IN SOMEONE'S HANDS

"EFFECT OF THE TRICK—You invite a person to take a pack of cards from the top of the deck at haphazard, and by testing the weight of the cards that remain in your hand, you divine how many cards have been taken. You have the cards that were taken counted to verify the estimate you have made of the quantity. Then you hand back these cards, placing them between the person's two hands and you increase their number according to the wish of the person who holds the cards.

EXPLANATION—Secretly count a certain number of cards on the top of the pack, we will suppose, eleven. Place the little finger underneath. In presenting the pack to someone, you ask her to take as many cards as she pleases. Push the eleven cards a little with the thumb, which puts them ready to be taken away so that they will be lifted naturally. Pretend to weigh the rest of the cards which you have in hand and you announce that eleven have been removed. While the person counts them, palm four cards in your hand, which you take from the remainder in your hands. When the count is finished, you say, in putting the four cards hidden in your hand on the eleven cards which are spread on the table, and as if merely to push them forward: 'Madam, take all these cards and hold them tightly in your two hands.' You ask her how many more she wishes you to pass, but warning her that only a small number should be demanded, such as three, four for example. The person to whom you address yourself, hearing these two numbers pronounced, is nearly always struck by them and, ordinarily, chooses the biggest, which is four. Then ruffling the pack by applying the thumb to one of the sides, you say: 'Madam, I· send them to you; count them and you will find fifteen.'

If, however, she demanded only three, you will say to her: 'Madam, give me one of them in order that it may show the way to the others which I shall send with it.'

When she has counted and found the fifteen, slide onto them another four cards in the same way, while saying: 'Madam, take them again in your hands; here are four more (you take them from the top of the pack) which I hold, and I am about to send them to you the same way.' Replace the four cards in the pack, which you ruffle as you did the first time, while saying: 'Count them again, madam, and you will find nineteen.'

This trick, well executed has a great effect. If it happens which is rarely, that two cards only are asked for, you say: 'Sir, do you want two also? That will be no harder for me.' He replies, naturally, 'Yes.' That makes up the four that are to be added.

Consider this, that in all tricks, it is necessary to seek out methods of coping with any embarrassing circumstances; with a little imagination they will be found; but, when such cases come unforeseen, it is necessary to have presence of mind."

Such was the original trick as explained by Ponsin and it will be noted that the expedients he gives are used to this very day, while the advice given in the last paragraph should be carefully noted by every performer.

Robert-Houdin, as with everything he touched, greatly improved the feat, giving it the form it has retained ever since, although the means of executing it have varied. Briefly, his method was this: He held in his right palm three cards of the same pattern as the pack to be used. The latter, in its original wrapper, he gave to a spectator with the request that the packet be opened and the cards counted. (French packs consist of thirty-two cards only.) The spectator then squared the pack, cut it into two portions, chose one and counted the cards it contained onto the table. Pushing the heap towards the spectator, Robert-Houdin added the three palmed cards as he requested the spectator to take the packet in his own hands and hold it tightly.

Picking up the remaining packet Robert-Houdin counted them onto the table, verifying the number held by the spectator, then he picked these cards up and, in handing them to a second person, he palmed off three cards. Using the three mystic words, Mene, Tekel, Upharsin, as a cabalistic formula, he ordered three cards to pass from one packet to the other and the passage of the cards was verified by the final count. Robert-Houdin says the trick produced "An extraordinary illusion. The verification of the number of the cards showing that the two heaps form a complete pack, seems to exclude all idea of palming off or adding any cards."

Since Robert-Houdin's day, many methods have been devised for bringing about the same effect by the use of various accessories such as envelopes, trays, etc., but it is doubtful if the trick is as effective as when done by a skilled operator using the cards only. The very latest method in which no cards are added or taken away by palming and no trick accessories are used, follows:

Infiltration

EFFECT—A spectator is invited to come forward. From a pack of red backed cards, ten cards are dealt deliberately onto the palm of his outstretched left hand and he at once closes his hand on these ten cards. As a precaution against any possible interference with them, a red silk handkerchief is thrown over his clenched hand, gathered around his wrist and secured there with a rubber band.

From a blue backed deck, ten cards are counted slowly, one by one, onto the palm of the same spectator's right hand and on these he immediately closes his fingers tightly. Over this hand a blue silk handkerchief is thrown and it also is secured with a rubber band around the wrist. At command three cards pass from the red backed packet in the spectator's left hand to the blue backed cards in his right hand. The rubber band and the red silk are removed and the red backed cards are counted slowly and carefully. There are seven only.

The rubber band and the blue silk are taken off his right hand and the cards are taken and dealt on it face up, there are thirteen. They are fanned backs outwards and three red backed cards show up amongst them.

PREPARATION—Take ten cards from a red backed pack and apply roughing fluid to the second and third, fifth and sixth, eighth and ninth, as follows: The second card on the back and the third card on the face, fifth card on the back and sixth card on the face, eighth card on the back and ninth card on. the face. Place these cards in that order on top of the red deck and put the deck in its case, first removing any three indifferent cards from the unprepared part of the pack.

Apply roughing fluid to the backs of these three red backed cards and to the face of three blue backed cards and put the pairs together, making three double cards with blue backs which can be separated at will. Place these double cards second, fifth and eighth from the top of the blue deck and replace the deck in its case. On your table place the two silk handkerchiefs, one red, one blue, two rubber bands, large enough to be stretched over the hands, and the two packs in their cases.

WORKING—Invite a spectator to come forward to help you. Place him on your left, the table being on your right and a little to the rear. Take the red deck from its case, make a false shuffle and then run the faces of the cards before the spectator's eyes. Remark that as the values of the cards have no bearing on the experiment, you will take the first that come to hand. Ask your helper to hold out his left hand, flat and palm upwards. Onto it deal, deliberately, the top ten cards, counting them aloud one by one. Owing to the arrangement of these cards the rough backs and faces of the second and third, the fifth and sixth and the eighth and ninth, will come together. Square the ten cards lightly with your right hand in such a way that the onlookers can always see that your hand is empty, and invite the spectator to grip the packet tightly. Put the pack on the table and pick up the red silk. Put it in the spectator's right hand and have him certify that it is ordinary and then spread it over his left hand himself. Let him gather the folds around his wrist, then you slip a rubber band over his fist and the silk down to his wrist. Ask him if he thinks it would be possible for anyone to abstract any of the cards without his consent. Naturally he replies in the negative. "That would be real magic, wouldn't it?" you say, and he agrees.

Take the blue backed pack, false shuffle and show the faces and backs. Ask your assistant to hold out his right hand, palm upwards, and again you deal ten cards, slowly and deliberately, counting them aloud. The second, fifth and eighth cards will be the double ones but this is not noticeable. Invite him to grip this packet tightly also. Lay the blue backed pack on the table and take the blue silk. Spread it out, show both sides and openly throw it over his right fist, gather the folds around his wrist and slip a rubber band over all as before. "Nothing could be added to those ten cards," you say to him, "without your knowing it?" And again he is positive that he has perfect control of both packets.

Announce to the audience what you propose to do, that is, to pass three cards from the packet of ten red backed cards in the spectator's left hand into the packet of ten blue backed cards in his right hand. The plot may very well be based on the infiltration of three red soldiers from the red camp to the blue camp and, unfortunately, such a plot is appropriate in these unhappy days. Or, you may simply order the three cards to pass invisibly. In any case, after the supposed passage has taken place, remove the rubber band and the red silk from the spectator's left hand, doing it very openly and letting it be seen that your hands are empty, and throw the red silk over your shoulder. Take the packet and deliberately count the cards as seven. The three pairs of rough cards cling together, making this count perfectly fair. Ask the spectator to drop the cards onto the red deck on your table.

Uncover the assistant's right hand, again doing it openly and showing the hands empty. Throw the blue silk over your shoulder, take the blue backed packet and count the cards slowly, face upwards, onto his right hand, separating the pairs of rough cards as you come to them, there are thirteen cards. Take them and fan them backs outwards showing the three red backed cards amongst them. Take these from the fan, counting one, two, three and show them dramatically. This is the climax, make the most of it. Shake hands with your helper, thank him and bow him off.

The arrangement of the trick is such that the performer can put the whole of his attention to the dramatic presentation of it. I have had it tested by several prominent magicians, both professional and amateur, under stage, club and drawing room conditions and their report is most enthusiastic.

REVERSE TRANSFER

DR. JACOB DALEY

EFFECT—A freely chosen card is placed in the magician's pocket, and a second card, also freely selected, is placed, reversed, in the middle of the pack. At command the cards instantly change places, the second card being found in the pocket and the first card reversed in the deck.

WORKING—Invite a spectator to shuffle the deck. On its return, riffle the outer ends of the deck, asking a spectator to call "Stop" at any moment he wishes. At the word, stop the riffle and cut the cards at that point. Make a double lift, showing the second card as being the card stopped at, suppose it is the five of Diamonds. Ask the spectator to remember it.

Turn the two cards face down as one, take off the top card, an indifferent card, and place it in your right trousers pocket, again calling it the five of Diamonds, and being careful not to let anyone get a glimpse of its face.

The card which was shown to the spectators, the five of Dia-monds in this case, now lies on the top of the deck. Undercut rather less than half the pack and make an overhand shuffle, in jogging the first card. Square the pack, insert the tip of the left little finger under the injogged card and hold a break there. Riffle the cards as be-fore, again inviting the spectator to call "Stop". Whenever he does so, drop the outer ends of the cards and lift off the top packet at the break which is found automatically with the right thumb at the rear end of the deck. Place this packet under the cards remaining in the right hand, thus bringing the five of Diamonds to the top.

Make a double lift and show the second card, suppose it is the Jack of Spades. Call its name and ask a second spectator to remember it. Under it is the five of Diamonds, also face up; take the two cards, as one, in the right hand and insert them in the middle of the pack. Push the cards in and, under cover of the visible Jack of Spades, push the card back of it, the five of Diamonds, flush with the rest of the pack, with the tip of the left second finger. At once pull the Jack of Spades round so that it protrudes from the right side of the deck for about half its width, Fig. 1. Drive the card flush with

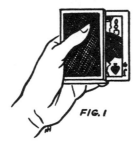

FIG. 1

the rest by successive pats with the right hand but hold a break at the spot by pressing on the back of the card with the tips of the left second and third fingers. Square the cards with the right hand, push the Jack of Spades into the right hand with the left fingers and palm it, that is to say, you execute the side slip.

Order the two cards to change places and immediately fan the pack widely with the right hand, backs out, and the first card, the five of Diamonds, shows up reversed in the spread. Thrust the right hand into your trousers pocket and bring out the palmed Jack of Spades, turning it over in the process, thus proving the instantaneous transposition of the two cards.

This trick is perfect for a quick effect with a borrowed deck since there can be no possible suspicion of the use of duplicate cards. Anyone who has had the good fortune to see Dr. Daley perform the trick will agree with this statement.

OPTICAL ILLUSION

R. M. JAMISON

A famous magician once claimed that he could duplicate with ordinary cards any effect brought about by the use of faked cards. The following startling effect of the kind which is usually done with the aid of double backed, double faced or rough cards, has been devised by my very ingenious friend, Mr. R. M. Jamison, using ordinary unprepared cards which can be handed out for examination immediately. This fact makes the trick a marvelous one for close intimate work, though it is equally effective for platform presentation.

Two red backed cards are required, a Queen of Spades and a Joker; three blue backed cards, Queen of Spades, Queen of Hearts and any indifferent card, also the remainder of a blue backed deck. To prepare for the trick: Place the red backed Joker on top of the blue backed deck, on it the indifferent blue backed card, on this the blue backed Queen of Spades, then the blue backed Queen of Hearts and, on top of all, the red backed Queen of Spades.

PRESENTATION—Pick up the pack and remark that you will use a blue backed pack of cards with one extra red backed card with red spots. Make a double lift and show the face of the Queen of Hearts and the red back of the supposed single card. Replace the two cards as one, then slide off the top card, the red backed Queen of Spades with the left thumb and set it against a support on your table, its back towards the spectators.

Again by the double lift, remove the next two top cards and show them as a blue backed Queen of Spades. Replace them on the pack and, as before, slide off the top card, the blue backed Queen of Hearts, setting it upright alongside the red backed card. Put the pack on the table.

Take the two cards in the right hand, holding them in readiness for the two card Monte move, see Fig. 1, and repeat the statement, "Red backed Queen of Hearts, red spots; blue backed Queen of Spades, black spots." Hold the cards by the top edges, backs outwards and fanned a little in readiness to slide them across one another as you spread them (the Monte move). Just before you make the

move, touch the back of the card nearest to you with the left forefinger, saying, "the blue back is the black spot card." Execute the
sleight and the left forefinger, barely moving, is placed against the
face of the card nearest you as you repeat, "blue back, black spot."

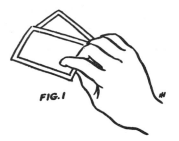

FIG. I

This is one of the most deceptive moves extant. The fact is that
the spectator's eyes cannot resist focussing on the performer's left
forefinger as it moves to touch the card and this disguises the movement of the cards entirely.

Now hold the two cards before your face, backs out, one in
each hand, and slowly turn the cards over in turn, repeating each
time, "Red back, red spots; blue back, black spots." Until someone
in the audience corrects you. Affecting astonishment, say: "I can't
account for the change, unless somehow the rubbing of the cards has
transferred the colors." Hand the two cards for examination.

"Now," you continue. "Let me show you something else, this
time with a card that has no spots to rub off, the blue backed Joker."
Take the pack, make a triple lift and show the Joker. Replace the
cards on top of the pack, slide off the top card, the blue backed Queen
of Spades, and insert it in the middle of the pack. Order the Joker
to mount to the top of the pack, make a double life and show it again.

Announce, "You will now see a real magical miracle." Pick
up the red backed card from the table, stroke the red back on the
blue back of the top card, supposedly the Joker, really the indifferent
card. Lay the red backed card down and cut the deck. Make a wide
fan, backs outwards, and a strange red card is seen amongst the
other cards. Remove it and lay it face down on the table. Spread
the cards, face outwards, and show that the Joker has vanished. Turn
the red backed card, it is the Joker. A baffling mystery, since you can
at once hand out the blue deck and the red Joker for the closest examination.

THINK-A-CARD

CHARLES HOPKINS

EFFECT—A card merely thought of is produced from the magicians pocket.

WORKING—The trick can be done with any pack but it is necessary to arrange the first ten cards in a known order. Any system can be used, Si Steppins, Eight Kings, or Nicola, and the arrangement can be made very easily right under the eyes of your audience, provided always that you are not furtive in your movements. It should be done while toying openly with the cards and while carrying on a conversation. We will suppose that you make use of the old Eight Kings set-up which is the simplest for this particular trick since you need pay no attention to the suits. A good plan is to take the necessary cards, one by one, beginning with the first card of the formula, an eight, and put them on the top. When you have thus taken all ten, make an overhand shuffle, running ten cards, injog the next card and shuffle off. Make a break at the injog, shuffle to the break, and throw the remaining cards on top. Follow with a riffle shuffle, false of course, and a blind cut, and no one will have any suspicion of a set-up. I remember on one occasion having seen a glib performer arranged the whole deck in the Nicola order while carrying on a brisk conversation. The audacity of the procedure prevented the onlookers from suspecting his maneuver.

Having set up the ten cards, make a false shuffle and several blind cuts, run the cards slowly before the eyes of a spectator, inviting him to merely think of one. When you have passed the fifth card, pause a moment and say: "Have you got one?" This will tend to make him fix on one promptly as you continue to pass the cards slowly.

When he says he has thought of a card, slip the tip of the left little finger under the ten arranged cards and square the pack. Take one of your business cards from your vest pocket, hand it to the spectator and instruct him to write the name of the card he has thought of on it and then lay the business card on the table, the written side downwards. So that there may be no suspicion of your getting any inkling of the writing, turn away while he writes.

Under cover of your body remove the cards above your left little finger and put them in your right trousers pocket. When the spectator tells you he has put the business card on the table, turn around shuffling the pack. Hand it to the spectator to shuffle and then put on the table. Ask him to cut the cards. As he does this you pick up the business card and, in the act of putting it on top of the cards left on the table after the cut, turn it over and read the name of the card written on it. At once take the cards the spectator cut off and put them on top of the business card, covering the writing and allowing only a small part of it to protrude. If this action is done casually, the fact that the writing was in view for a moment will never be noticed.

Put your right hand in your trousers pocket, run over the sequence of the ten cards, find the thought card and pull it up into the top corner of the pocket. In the meantime you recapitulate what has been done. You say that it would be a very remarkable thing for him to have cut at the very card he thought of but you will do something still more wonderful. You will take the card he cut at out of the pack and put it invisibly into your pocket. Make a pretense of taking a card from the pack and passing it to your trousers pocket.

Have the spectator take the business card out of the pack, read aloud the name of the card as if you did not know its name. Then slowly bring the card from the pocket at the tips of the fingers, turn it and show that it is the right one.

The trick is particularly interesting from the fact that by subtlety and misdirection only a fine effect is obtained without the use of sleights. Occasional use of such tricks tends to allay suspicion when you really employ sleights.

ZISKA IMPROVED

GERALD KOSKY

EFFECT—While the magician's back is turned a spectator is invited to think of a number between one and ten, cut the pack and transfer cards, one by one, to the number thought of, from the lower part of the pack to the upper portion, i. e. the part cut off. He is then to look at the last card thus transferred, remember what it is, replace it, complete the cut and square the cards carefully. The magician then divines the number mentally selected, and the noted card, in a mysterious way and without asking any questions.

WORKING—A key card is necessary and it must be marked near the top right hand corner and the bottom left hand corner so that it can be found easily when the cards are spread face down from right to left. When using a borrowed deck an opportunity can readily be found for putting light pencil dots in the required positions when your back is turned in the course of a trick, or a thumb writer, a daub, or even a corner crimp, can be used to make the key card.

A set-up must be made of ten cards, a sequence running from a ten down to an ace, of any cards of mixed suits, and this set-up packet must lie under the key card so that the ace is the bottom card of the deck. This arrangement can be made very easily while toying with the deck and carrying on a conversation, see Think-a-card, p. 39, or the Barnyard shuffle can be used, (More Card Manipulations No. 2, p. 23.)

The ten cards being in position at the bottom of the deck, with the key card immediately above them, secretly crimp the inner end of the packet of ten cards by squeezing them with the left hand, the results being shown in Fig. 1. Put the pack on the table and show

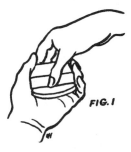

FIG. I

the spectator what he is to do. First he is to cut the pack into two portions about equal. You do this. Then he is to think of a number between one and ten. You suppose, for example, that he thinks of three. He is to transfer three cards from the lower section to the other part, and you do this. Next he is to look at the last card so transferred, note what it is, replace it, complete the cut and square the cards. All of which you do. Point out that by this means the spectator will have fixed on a number and a card which will be known only to himself and that the noted card will be buried in the pack.

Pick up the pack and say to the spectator: "Remember you must first cut the pack so," and you cut at the crimp casually, as if merely to impress on him what he is to do. Complete the cut, seizing the opportunity to obliterate the crimp, and put the pack down. The position now is this—on the top is the sequence of ten cards, from the ten to the ace, and on the bottom is your key card.

You turn away. The spectator cuts the pack and we will suppose that he thinks of the number five. He transfers five cards from the lower part to the other portion, that is to say onto the set-up, and looks at the last card. Finally he completes the cut, bringing the key card on top of the card just noted, and he squares the deck.

He notifies you that he is ready, you turn and take the pack. You may now execute a complete false shuffle and several blind cuts, or merely make several complete cuts. Spread the cards in a long line on the table from right to left so that the top right hand corner of each card will be exposed. Fig. 2. The eleventh card from the

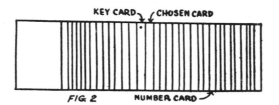

FIG. 2   NUMBER CARD

key card, counting towards the right, will denote by its spots the number the spectator mentally selected. You can use any method you like to pick out this card. For example, you may take hold of the spectator's left hand with your left hand, then pass your right hand slowly over the line of cards from left to right and drop your forefinger on the eleventh card after the key card as if by some impulse transmitted from him.

In any case, push this eleventh card out of the line and leave it face down. Pick up the line of cards from the right hand end in the manner described on page 12, dropping the right thumb on the card below the key card and transferring this right hand packet to the top in the action. The key card is thus brought to the bottom of the pack and the top card of the pack will be the card noted by the spectator. Square the pack, take it in the right hand between the thumb and fingers at the ends and, in placing the cards on the table, palm the top card by the one hand method. (Card Manipulations No. 1, p. 2.)

Casually place both hands in your trousers pockets as you ask the spectator: "Would you be surprised if I have divined the number you thought of? You would? Well, I not only know it but I have picked out one card which has that very same number of spots. There it is. To show that we have made no arrangement about the matter, will you name your number? Five? Turn the card face up yourself. You see I read your thoughts correctly. Now what card did you note? The.............. of .... I'm afraid you have made a mistake. That card is not in the pack." Take the pack in your right hand and spread it widely on the table face up. "Knowing that card to be an unlucky one for me, I put it in my pocket before we began the trick." In your gestures let it be seen that you hand is empty, thrust it into your pocket and bring out the card.

When using your own deck, a short card with the corners marked makes the trick very easy to work, but it is more surprising when done, as above, with a borrowed deck. The late Ziska's use of this principle will be found on page 38 of the "Art of Magic."

THREE CARDS AND A BANK NOTE (Bill)

DR. RICHARD ROWE

EFFECT—Three spectators draw cards, note them and each places his card in an envelope and seals it. The pack is replaced in its case an a fourth spectator puts it in his pocket. A dollar bill, or a bank note, is borrowed and also placed in an envelope and sealed. The magician places the envelopes in turn against his forehead and reads the names of the cards and the number of the bill. The envelopes are returned to the spectators for verification but they are found to be empty. The spectator holding the card case, opens it and in the middle of the deck he finds the missing bill wrapped around the three chosen cards. The number of the bill is checked and it proves to be the one called by the magician.

PREPARATION—Three cards are wrapped in a bill, the number of which the magician memorizes or writes on his thumb nail. This packet is placed in a card case underneath the pack on the top of which are three duplicates of the cards. Several cards should be removed from the pack to make room for this packet.

A tray on your table has four closed, empty envelopes under it and is so placed that the rear edges of the tray and the envelopes overlap the edge of the table so that both tray and envelopes can be lifted cleanly. Two table mats, obtainable at the dime stores, glued back to back, making the top and bottom alike in appearance, serve the purpose very well. Also on the table you have a packet of envelopes similar to those under the tray.

WORKING—Take the pack from its case, leaving the prepared packet inside, and put the case in your right outside coat pocket. Make a false shuffle and force the three duplicate cards on three spectators. Hand the packet of envelopes to the first spectator, telling him to choose one, place his card in it, seal it and hand the rest of the envelopes to the second person that he may do likewise. This man hands the remaining envelopes to the third spectator who also takes an envelope, puts his card in it and seals it.

While this is being done, take out the card case, place the remainder of the pack in it in such a way that the prepared packet will be in the middle of the deck, an easy matter. Close the flap of the case and hand the case to another spectator to put in his inside breast pocket.

Borrow a dollar bill and have it placed in an envelope. As the owner closes and seals the flap, pick up the tray with your right hand, the thumb on top and gripping the four envelopes underneath it with the fingers. Fig. 1. Collect the four envelopes from the spectators on the tray, stacking them under the thumb. Take the remaining envelopes in your left hand, turn and go to your table. Under cover of your body, turn the tray over in this manner: Move the right first finger to the top of the tray and with it grip the four envelopes there, releasing the thumb, Fig. 2, move the thumb underneath the tray, gripping the envelopes at the bottom, release the second and third fingers, turn the tray over and close the three fingers below it. You now hold the tray in exactly the same way as before, but the empty envelopes are under your thumb and the spectators' envelopes are underneath, gript by the fingers. In the action, which takes but a moment, keep the right elbow pressed close to the side and the left hand with the other envelopes in full view. Drop the surplus envelopes on the table so that they scatter a little and put the

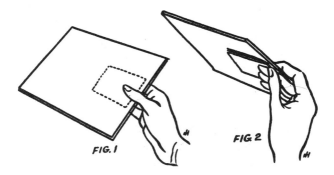

FIG. 1   FIG. 2

tray down on top of them, releasing the four spectators' envelopes which join them imperceptibly.

Take one of the envelopes from the tray, place it against your forehead and announce the name of one of the three cards in the usual mindreading fashion, color first, then value, then suit, and have it acknowledged. Do the same with two more envelopes, pretending to feel for the ones with cards in them.

Take the last envelope, hold it to your forehead and read the number of your own bill which you memorized, at the same time writing the figures boldly with black crayon on the address side of the envelope. Note that the writing must begin at the right hand end of the envelope and continue in reverse fashion. A few minutes' practice before a mirror will make this easy to do.

Give the four envelopes back to the spectators for them to verify the cards and the number of the bill. They report that the envelopes are empty. Pretend to be surprised, then have the fifth spectator take the case from his pocket and remove the cards. In the middle of the pack he finds three cards wrapped in a bill. Let him call the names of the three cards one by one and have them acknowledged by the spectators who drew them. Then have him read out the number of the bill and check it with the numbers you wrote on the envelope. Check.

The technical part of the trick is easy and the performer is free to bend all his energy towards giving a dramatic presentation. Dr. Rowe never fails to make a hit with the trick.

Synopsis

Memorize number of bill, wrap around three cards, put in card case.

Close flaps of four envelopes, place under tray on table.

Force three duplicate cards, have them placed in envelopes.

Put pack in case; place in spectator's pocket.

Borrow bill; have it put in an envelope.

Collect envelopes on tray; switch them.

Put envelopes to forehead in turn; read contents.

Return envelope to spectators; found empty.

Pack removed from case; cards and bill found.

Check cards and number of bill.

THE SCORE CARD SCORES

FRED BRAUE

EFFECT—A spectator freely selects a card from any deck, notes it, replaces it and the cards are thoroughly shuffled. He then thrusts the bridge score card into the deck and infallibly locates his card.

WORKING—The trick begins in the routine way, a card is chosen by a spectator, noted, replaced and brought to the top; a false shuffle and blind cut are made to convince everyone that the card is really lost amongst the others. If you feel that you must show that the card is not at the top nor the bottom, do not overwork the double lift. Send the card second from the bottom by the overhand shuffle and show the bottom card, turn the pack and show several cards at the top. Shuffle overhand again and bring the card to the top, following this with a blind cut.

Give the score card to the spectator and invite him to thrust it into the end of the deck, which you hold in your left hand, face downwards, at any point he pleases. You warn him in all seriousness that, while he will imagine he does this of his own volition, you will compel him to insert the score card either above or below the card he chose.

Accordingly the spectator thrusts the score card into the end of the deck and you take care that about one-third of its length remains protruding, Fig. 1. Grip the cards above the score card with your right hand, between the thumb at the lower left corner and the

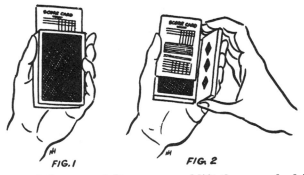

FIG. 1   FIG. 2

second finger at the upper left corner, and lift these cards deliberately bookwise, Fig. 2, so that the top card of this packet, the chosen card, rests against the left fingers in position for the regular back slip

Execute this sleight, pulling off the top card with the left fingers and folding it onto the top card of the portion which remains in the left hand. In the action both hands swing a little to the right and turn over so that, at the end of the movement, the right hand holds its packet face upwards, showing the face of the card that was above the score card and the left hand has its back uppermost, its forefinger pointing to the exposed card of the right hand packet, Fig. 3. "Is that your card?" you ask. "No? Well that was the card above the scorecard, so the card below it must be yours."

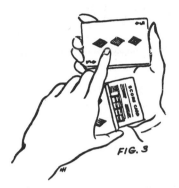

Hold the right hand packet between the thumb and third finger at the ends, freeing the first and second fingers. Keep the left hand in the same position and with the tips of the right first and second fingers draw away the score card, Fig. 4. Turn the left hand over

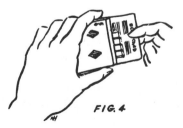

and show the packet lying face down on it. Have the chosen card named, push it off the side of the packet a little with the left thumb and flip it over, face upwards, with the score card.

The moves blend very nicely and are apparently predicated by necessity, thus making them natural. This is the most effective of all the locator card stabs and it makes a strong impression on the onlookers, particularly if used in a four or five card Location routine. It is best to use the score card as the locator card, both sides being printed there can be no question in the spectator's mind of an exchange of cards or other skullduggery. I recommend the trick strongly even to that mythical personage . . . . the most fastidious performer.

THE CURRY TURN OVER CHANGE

There can be no doubt that this sleight, first explained in "More Card Manipulations No. 2," of this series, will become one of the standard sleights, an indispensable part of the equipment of the up-to-date card worker. From amongst the many suggestions for its use that have been sent in, room can be found here for one only, an adaptation of the popular "Do AS I Do" trick, by Mr. Jerry Nadell.

As in the regular version two packs are required, one with a red back, the other blue backed. To prepare for the trick, place the Ace of Diamonds, for example, on the top of the blue deck; then from the red backed pack take out its Ace of Diamonds and place it, reversed, on the bottom of the blue deck. Lay the two decks on the table.

It is necessary that you appear to give the spectator a choice of the packs and a simple way to do this is to ask him to touch one of them. If he touches the red pack, say: "You choose that one? Then I'll take the blue pack." If, however, he touches the blue pack, say: "You want me to use that pack for the trick? Very well, you hold the other one." In any case the spectator must get the red deck.

Instruct him to do as you do and you make a riffle shuffle. In order to avoid any chance exposure of the red backed Ace of Diamonds on the bottom of your blue backed deck, let the deck remain on the table, cut the upper half with your right hand and with the left thumb lift about three quarters of the lower packet in readiness for the riffle shuffle. By this means the reversed red card and several other cards are not raised from the table. Next instruct your victim to cut his cards and, for your part, execute the Erdnase cut, Fig. 1, sending the top card, the Ace of Diamonds, to the middle

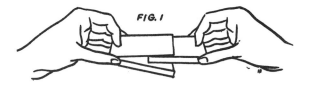

FIG. I

and hold a break above that card with the tip of your left little finger.

Now explain that you are going to select one of the cards from your deck. Fan your deck, select one card (The Ace of Diamonds) and drop it face down on the table without showing what card it is. Invite the spectator to do exactly the same with his deck, i. e.: fan it out, make a free selection of ANY card and, without looking at it, place it face down on the table to the left of your card. Impress upon the spectator that your card was selected FIRST—his card SECOND, yet the simultaneous actions have compelled him to draw the same card as yours. Turn over the two cards simultaneously, your card with the right hand and his card with your left hand—executing the Curry turn over sleight to change his indifferent card for the reversed red backed Ace of Diamonds on the bottom of your blue backed deck.

The action leaves a reversed red backed card on the bottom of your blue backed deck. It is a simple matter to palm this in your right hand as you turn the deck to spread the cards face up on the table. Immediately afterwards pick up the red pack, adding the palmed card to it, turn the pack and spread it also face upwards. Positive proof is thus given that there are no duplicate cards and that both packs are ordinary. You are then ready to proceed with any other desired trick.

This trick is probably the most convincing form of the popular "Follow Me" effect in that an apparent miracle takes place—due to the speed and clean-cut presentation. The fact that the red card is turned over with the hand holding the blue pack apparently eliminates any possibility of the magician manipulating the cards.

A CUR(R)I-OUS PREDICTION

PAUL CURRY

EFFECT—A pack of cards, any pack, after being shuffled by a spectator is taken by the performer, who runs his eye over the faces and returns the pack to the spectator. While the spectator, at the performer's request, holds the pack face up behind his back, the performer writes something on a piece of paper which he folds and places in the spectator's breast pocket. Standing directly in front of the spectator the performer instructs him to remove a card from the face up pack and turn it face down pushing it into the pack after he has done so. The cards are brought forward and are retained by the performer while the spectator reads aloud the name of the card written on the paper. In this case let us say that the card predicted is the Ace of Hearts. Turning sideways the performer fans the cards so that both he and the spectator may see the faces as the performer fans thru with the remark that they will find the Ace and see what it has to do with the trick. Strangely enough the Ace is not to be found among the face up cards. "Well," remarks the performer. "Since it isn't to be found among the face-up cards there is only one possibility; it must be the one card you turned face-down." Saying this he slowly turns over the one reversed card and reveals it to be the Ace in question.

METHOD—The effect depends upon two moves. The first, if it may be termed a move, is to reverse the lowermost card of the deck, when the pack is in a face-up position.

The cards are shuffled and given to the performer who runs over the faces noting, as he does so, the topmost (rear) card of the pack. The name of this card is written on the paper which is folded and placed in the spectator's breast pocket. As this is being done the left hand drops to the side and the fingers of the left hand turn the top noted card face-up on the pack. This is not at all difficult as it is well covered. (The thumb pushes the card forward and the card is pivoted over into a face-up position.) As you bring your hand up, reverse the entire deck so that the deck is face-up with the noted card face-down on the bottom of the deck. The pack is handed face-up to the spectator who places it behind his back and turns one of the cards face-down which he inserts in the pack and squares up the deck. The cards, upon being returned to the performer, are held in the left hand while the spectator reads the prediction.

After remarking that he will find the card just read the performer runs the cards slowly from the left to the right hand with the spectator taking a Kibitzer position beside the performer. This is continued until the spectator's reversed card is arrived at. The fan is broken at this point, the spectator's reversed card being retained as the bottom card of the right hand half fan. "Since we haven't come to the predicted card as yet", remarks the performer, " we'll just place the card you reversed at the bottom of the pack and out of the way for a moment."

It is at this point that the basic move of the entire effect takes place. Both hands are holding partly fanned packets. The left hand closes its packet. The right hand approaches, with its packet still partly fanned, pushing, the bottom, or reversed card, partly out from the rest. As this is done the left middle, fourth and little fingers open to receive this card on the bottom of the left hand packet. The left hand packet is now held by the thumb and forefinger at the outer end, the thumb on top and the forefinger underneath. Fig. 1. The protruding reversed card is brought in beneath the left hand packet —below the forefinger and above the three extended fingers. When in this position, which should only be for a second or less, the

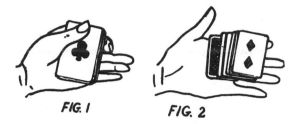

FIG. 1   FIG. 2

fingers of the right hand withdraw the reversed card smartly back underneath the right hand fan. At this moment the left hand opens wide all its fingers tilting the hand slightly and causing the cards to slide forward onto the extended left fingers exposing the reverse (predicted) card at the bottom of the left packet. Fig. 2. Keeping the spectator's reversed card hidden at the bottom of the right hand packet, the performer continues to fan the cards in his search for the Ace. Finally all the cards have been fanned into the right hand. Pattering along the lines previously mentioned the reversed card on the bottom of the pack is turned up and the effect is completed as outlined.

Smoothly done and properly synchronized the illusion is that the reversed card has never been out of sight!

It should be noted that this move lends itself to other uses, for instance: With the cards face down, and the lower most card reversed, the pack is spread in a face-down fan as you invite a spectator to touch one. The touch card is flipped face-up by the right hand fan, and is placed, face-up, at the bottom of the right hand fan. As in the previous effect this reversed card is apparently placed at the bottom of the left hand packet, but in reality is pulled back beneath the cards in the right hand. In this case the left hand does not allow its cards to slide forward as the change would be noticed in the face-up cards. Instead, the left hand packet is turned over, the reversed card at the bottom is pushed off by the thumb and received onto the bottom of the right hand fan where it is retained by the fingers underneath. The left packet is turned face-down again, placed beneath the right hand cards and the entire pack, squared. A tap, flick or riffle and the cards are fanned showing the selected card reversed in the center.

THE QUESTION IS . . . . . .

PAUL MORRIS

To get the full effect from this trick you must be able to palm a card by the one hand method (Card Manipulations No. 1, p. 2.) Hence the title "The question is . . . . . . " If the reader has not already mastered this sleight I strongly recommend him to do so. It enhances the effect of any trick in which a single card has to be palmed from the top of the pack and this trick gives a good example of its use.

Any pack can be used and you obtain the assistance of two spectators, whom we will call A and B. Have them stand a little in front of and facing you, A to the left and B to the right. Hand the pack to B asking him to shuffle the cards to his own satisfaction. This done, take the pack and allow A to make a free selection of one card. When he has noted it, suppose it is the Ace of Spades, have the card returned to the pack, control it, bringing it to the top and make a thorough shuffle, leaving it there. Lay the pack face down on your left palm, the fingers extended. Ask A to remember his card and, with a casual gesture, let it be seen that your right hand is empty.

Bring your right hand over the pack, grasp it between the tips of the right thumb, at the inner end, and the four fingers at the outer end; lift it and hand it to B and in the action palm the top card, A's card, the Ace of Spades, by the one hand method. "Now," you say to B, "Will you select any card you please and place it on the top of the pack, after noting what it is."

This done, take the pack from him, secretly adding the palmed card, and turn to A, continuing, "Let us see what kind of a magician you will make. Your own card has been lost in the pack. No one knows what it is but yourself. Mr. B's card is here on the top." Make the double lift and show, for example, the two of Diamonds. "That is right, isn't it?" you say and B acquiesces. Turn the two cards face down, as one card. Take off the top card, the Ace of Spades, holding it face down in your right hand, turn the left hand over bringing the pack face upwards and hand it to A, saying: "Will you hold the cards face up and push this card . : . . . (hesitate a moment, turn the card towards yourself, being careful that no one else sees its face) the two of Diamonds, right here into the middle of the deck?" Insert the card about an inch yourself and let him push it flush with the rest of the cards.

The deck is now face up in A's hand. Have him hold his hand out and say to him: "If I turn the pack face down so, naturally B's card will be face upwards. That's right, isn't it?" As you suit the action to the words, let it be seen that your hands are empty. Take the pack with the right hand, as before, in position for the right hand palm and give it to B, palming the top card, the two of Diamonds in transit. Continue, "I noticed a rather incredulous smile on your face when I told A he would become a magician. Well, I have complete confidence in him and to prove it I am going to make you a present of this five dollar bill," thrust your right hand into your trousers pocket, leave the palmed card there and bring out a bill, "If you can remove that face up two of Diamonds from the pack. Try."

B goes through the pack and finds the face-up Ace of Spades which A claims is his card, but fails to find any two of Diamonds. Continue, "Why, he is a greater magician than I thought. He has reversed his own card. Do you know what he did with your card? He slipped it into my pocket when you weren't looking. Here it is." Bring out the two of Diamonds from your pocket.

Thank your two assistants and, as they leave, say to A, "You won't tell him how you did it, will you?"

PSYCHO-CARDITIS

Nothing New But the Presentation

DR. H. WALTER GROTE

EFFECT—Any pack can be used and it is first shuffled by the spectator. The performer gazed intently into his eyes for a few moments, then writes something on a slip of paper, folds it and gives it to the spectator to put in his pocket.

The spectator cuts the pack into two piles and selects one, while the performer takes the other. The spectator deals his cards face down, one card at a time, until he wishes to stop and then turns the next card face up. According to the number of spots on this card, the performer deals from his packet a correspondng number of cards. The last card on being turned face up proves to be the card previously written down by the ·performer.

WORKING—Ask a spectator to shuffle the pack. When he is satisfied that the cards are well mixed, take the pack from him and lay it on the table, getting a glimpse of the bottom card in the process. Take a pencil and paper from your pocket, gaze into the spectator's eyes and, after appropriate business, write down the name of the glimpsed card. Fold the paper and give it to the spectator to put into his pocket.

Turn to the table and ask the spectator to cut the cards into two equal packets. Invite him to touch one. If he touches the one with the glimpsed card on the bottom, you say: "I am to take that one," and you pick it up, while he takes the other one. If, on the other hand, he touches the packet he has just cut off, you say: "You choose that one? Take it and I will take the other." In any case you pick up the packet with the known bottom card. Invite him to shuffle his cards and you do the same with yours, being careful of course, not to disturb the bottom card.

Ask the spectator then to deal one card at a time, face down, stop on any card he pleases and turn the next card face up. While he does this gaze at him intently as if you were exercising some kind of mental control. Let us suppose that he turns up a six spot, you say: "I shall now deal from my packet down to the sixth card." Deal five· cards face down and say to him, "Before we turn the next card, please read aloud what I have written on the slip of paper in your pocket."

As soon as he begins to unfold the paper you side slip the known card to the top of the packet in your hand and immediately lay the packet on the table. When he has read your prediction, ask him to turn the next card, which, of course, proves to be the correct one. If properly presented this is a veritable "stunner."

Note: To facilitate the side slip of the bottom card I would suggest that, after dealing one less than the number of spots on the spectator's card, you take your packet by the left corners between the second finger and thumb of the right hand and make a gesture with it towards the spectator as you invite him to take the slip and read it aloud. In replacing the cards in your left hand it is an easy matter to side slip the bottom card with the left fingers into the right palm. A moment later take the packet with your right hand, adding the palmed card, and put the packet on the table in front of the spectator.

The following method, producing the same effect by a different means is by Mr. John Crimmins, Jr.

Another method employing the faced deck principle, explained on page 7, will be found quite practical. Glimpse the third card from the bottom, or shuffle your glimpsed card to that position. reverse these three cards on the bottom so that the glimpsed card is the bottom card. This can be accomplished while the spectator is shuffling his packet. An elastic band can now be snapped around your packet and it is laid on the table with the faced cards to the bottom. When you pick up the packet to count, hold it in the same position, and draw the cards off the top until you come to one less than the number designated. Under cover of the misdirection explained in the above paragraph, you reverse the packet and hold it out to the spectator allowing him to withdraw the next card—which will be the correct one.

More Card Manipulations

SERIES 4

Illustrations by Donna Allen

CONTENTS

CHAPTER I. SLEIGHTS

CHAPTER II. FLOURISHES

CHAPTER III. TRICKS

CHAPTER I.   SLEIGHTS

HUGARD CARD CONTROL

There is always room for a new method of controlling a card after it has been replaced in the pack, provided that the method is an easy and indetectable one.   I have had the following sleight tested by experts and also by novices and it has won unanimous approval.

We will suppose that a card has been chosen, noted and replaced in the pack by a spectator, that you have the pack in your left hand and have secured a break above the chosen card with the left little finger : to bring the card to the top secretly, proceed as follows :

1.   Grasp the left corners of the pack between the top joints of the right second finger at the outer end and the right thumb at the inner end and turn the pack upwards to a vertical position, its lower side resting on the middle joints of the left fingers and the little finger retaining the break.   In the action move the left thumb out of the way and then let its tip rest on the face of the bottom card near the middle.   Place the forefinger against the outer end of the pack, Fig. 1.

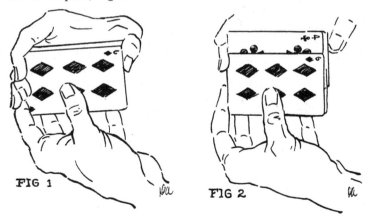

FIG 1   FIG 2

2.   Holding the pack rather loosely, press lightly on the face card with the left thumb and on the back of the chosen card with the left little finger and lift the inner ends of all the other cards by turning the right hand outwards, thus raising the right thumb and the inner top corner of the pack about an inch and a half, Fig. 2.

3. Lift the pack upwards until it clears the two cards held back by the left thumb and little finger, at the same time closing the left fingers against the back of the chosen card. The left forefinger at the outer end of the pack keeps the two cards in alignment.

4. Shuffle the pack overhand onto the face card; on completion of the shuffle the desired card will be the top card of the deck ready to be dealt with in any way required for the trick in hand. It will generally be found advisable to repeat the overhand shuffle with the pack in the same position, retaining the top card by a light pressure of the left fingers on its back.

This sleight is very useful for bringing a lost card or a needed card secretly to the bottom. For instance, suppose you need a nine at the top of the pack; you have simply to run over the cards, find a nine, insert the left little finger at its face, shuffle overhand, using the control, and so bringing the card to the bottom. Then by means of a second overhand shuffle you bring it to the top of the pack.

THE BOTTOM PALM SIMPLIFIED

Nowadays when a smattering of magicians' trickeries has been so widely spread that the word *palm* in the conjuring sense has become a commonplace in the jargon of reporters, many people are quick to suspect and closely watch a performer's right hand. For some unknown reason, however, the magician is never suspected of palming with his left hand, even by those who know a good deal about card sleights. The ability to palm cards with the left hand is, therefore, a very valuable weapon in the conjurer's armory of sleights.

The method explained by Erdnase, in which a packet of cards is twisted from the bottom of the pack by the right little finger and then pressed into the palm by the right thumb is a difficult one and therefore but little used. By the following modification the twisting action of the right little finger is eliminated and the sleight becomes a very easy one to acquire.

In palming with the left hand the cards are stolen from the bottom of the deck and it is rarely necessary to count the cards to be palmed. For instance, suppose that the four aces are on the bottom and you wish to palm them in the left hand with a view to replacing them in that position after the pack has been shuffled by a spectator. Obviously, it will make no difference if you palm five or six cards, or even more, since when they are replaced the aces will still be on the bottom. The one rule to follow is to palm *not less than* the number required and this can be assured by feel alone.

Here are the moves:

1. Hold the pack, between the right second and third fingers at the middle of the outer end and the right thumb at the inner end, in the fork

of the left thumb, the thumb lying across the back and the tips of the left fingers resting against the left side, level with the top card, Fig. 1.

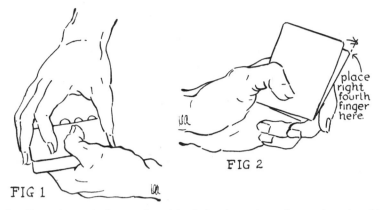

FIG 1

FIG 2

place right fourth finger here.

2. Run the pack forward and back in the action of squaring the sides, then again well forward so that the tip of the left second finger rests on the inner right corner; with this finger tip pull down the corners of the desired cards and, at the same time, twist the outer end of the pack about half an inch to the left, Fig. 2.

This action causes the upper right corner of the desired packet to project from the side of the deck; press the top joint of the right little finger against the end of this packet, thus concealing the projection. Hold a break between the pack and the packet at the inner end with the right thumb, Fig. 3.

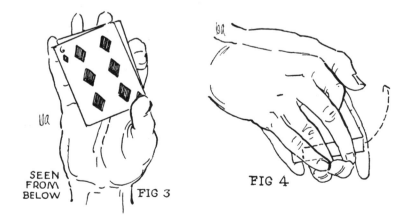

SEEN FROM BELOW   FIG 3

FIG 4

3. Retain the pack in this grip in the right hand and remove the left hand, making with it a casual gesture incidental to your patter and carelessly allowing it to be seen empty.

4. Bring the hands together in such a way that the left hand rests momentarily along the length of the pack, Fig. 4. Instantly press the top joint of the left little finger against the protruding corner of the desired packet, thus pressing its opposite diagonal corner against the base of the left thumb; twist the pack upwards towards the left, placing it in the fork of the left thumb in exactly the same position as in item 1. Close the left fingers on the packet, palming it, and run the pack back and forth, squaring its sides.

The whole action is exceptionally easy and the cards can be palmed in a flash.

TO SHUFFLE OR NOT TO SHUFFLE

The only method for bringing a chosen card to the top or bottom of the pack given by the early textbooks is the pass. Even in *Modern Magic,* although several methods of making the pass are explained, no substitute for it is given. This applies also to *Sleight of Hand* by Sachs who gives specific instruction to the neophyte to proceed immediately to an overhand shuffle after the pass is made. In recent years many substitutes for the pass have been devised and in almost all of them the immediate use of the shuffle is either necessary or considered advisable.

The question arises, is it good practice to execute a shuffle directly after the pass has been made? Sachs' idea was that, even though the spectators might notice that some movement had been made, the subsequent apparently thorough mixing of the cards would annul any suspicion that the conjurer could have kept track of the chosen card. Many experts nowadays contend that this course is wrong and tends to destroy the conviction of the spectator that the card he chose has actually been lost in the pack.

They maintain that if, immediately after the replacment of the chosen card, the pack is openly squared and laid aside for a moment or two without being shuffled or manipulated in any way, the spectator will be satisfied that his card has really been buried amongst the other cards. Its subsequent discovery then becomes somewhat of a miracle.

There are several ruses whereby this contention can be put to the test; the bottom card can be crimped at the inner right corner and an undercut made for the return of the card, thus bringing the crimped card above it; a jog may be made or the bridge may be used. Again, here is an easy method whereby control of a card can be retained even though the deck is honestly shuffled immediately after its return and then laid on the table.

1.   A card having been selected, make a short overhand shuffle as it is being noted, then square the pack.

2.   Undercut about half the deck by pulling out the lower portion, gripping the inner corners of the packet between the right thumb and finger tips.   Extend the left hand towards the spectator, inviting him to replace his card on top of the cards therein and focus your attention on this action.

3.   At the same moment squeeze the inner end of the packet in your right hand with the thumb and second finger, slightly bridging the cards, Fig. 1.

FIG. 1

4.   As soon as the chosen card has been placed on the cards in your left hand, slap the packet in the right hand on top and immediately square the pack very openly.

5.   Take the pack in the right hand, face outwards, at the upper corners between the thumb and second fingers, forefinger on the upper side, and tap the lower side on the table.

6.   Next take it by the sides with the left hand and then again with the right hand by the ends between the thumb and second finger, the forefinger on the upper side, and tap the lower side on the table.   Finally lay the pack face down on the table, the bridged end towards you.

7.   Rub your hands together or pull back your cuffs a trifle as you make some remark about what has been done, then pick up the pack.   Hold it in the left hand as for dealing and with the right thumb and fingers square the

ends. The tiniest bridge can be found by rubbing the ball of the thumb along the inner end without looking at the cards. Cut at the bridge, execute a riffle shuffle letting the top card of the left hand drop last and you have the chosen card on the top of the pack.

From first to last every action has been perfectly natural. Even if the reader is wedded to the idea of shuffling immediately after the pass has been made, this method should be used occasionally as a change of pace to throw the spectators off the scent.

Another easy and effective method is to use a reversed card on the bottom of the pack as a locator; in this case you proceed as follows:

1. Reverse the face card of the deck. Have a card chosen. Undercut or run-cut with a Hindu shuffle, dropping the reversed card above the chosen card on its return to the pack.

2. Square the pack very openly and lay it on the table.

3. When you retake the pack, you have merely to make the Charlier pass and you have the reversed card at the bottom, the chosen card at the top.

This leaves you with the necessity of righting the reversed card. The following simple but highly ingenious method has been devised by my friend, Mr. Fred Braue, for this purpose.

Cut the pack at about the middle and drop the packet, face upwards on the table. Cut off about half the remaining cards and drop them face upwards on the first packet. Place the remainder on the top, face down, as if inadvertently, then slide off the face down cards and turn them over. Thus the reversed card again faces the same way as the other cards and no sleight has been necessary to correct it. This is a good ruse to know and particular note should be taken.

THE RIFFLE FORCE

We will suppose that the card to be forced is at the top of the pack. Proceed as follows:

1. Undercut a little more than half the pack and execute an overhand shuffle, jogging the first card in the action.

2. Square the pack with the right hand, forming a break under the jogged card and holding it with the tip of the left little finger.

3. Grip the upper packet, that is to say, the cards above the break, with the right thumb at the inner end and the right second and third fingers at the outer end, the tip of the left forefinger resting lightly on the back.

4. Bend the left forefinger under the pack and with the left thumb riffle the outer left corners of the cards, calling attention to the action, Fig. 1. Say that you will repeat it and invite a spectator to call *stop* whenever he wishes.

5. Repeat the riffle. At the call of *stop,* cease riffling, press the point of the left thumb downwards slightly on the corners of the cards still below it and with the right hand carry off the whole packet above the break to a distance of five or six inches. Do not lift the packet, take it away sideways, Fig. 2.

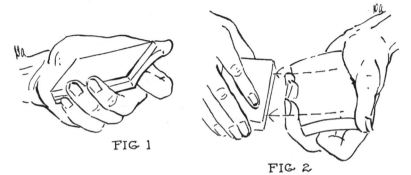

FIG. 1

FIG. 2

6. Extend the left hand towards the spectator, inviting him to take the top card of the packet in that hand. It is an easy matter to contrive to stop the riffle fairly close to the bottom of the packet above the break, thus avoiding any noticeable discrepancy in the size of the packet removed. Keep the left thumb tip pressing down on the corner of the lower packet as you extend it towards the spectator. The few cards not riffled slide away imperceptibly.

Some performers prefer to hold the pack in position for the thumb riffle in the left hand at about shoulder height, the back of the hand upwards. When the riffle is stopped, the left hand is turned over bringing the pack face downwards and the right hand takes away the packet above the break as described above.

This force is an easy and convincing one, the preliminary shuffle satisfies the spectator that you cannot have any particular card under control.

THE COUNT FORCE

We will suppose that the card to be forced, the four of diamonds, is on the top of the pack and that you have executed a false shuffle, retaining it in that position.

1.   Hold the pack in the left hand as for dealing and invite a spectator to call any number. Let us say that the answer is *nine*.

2.   Take the cards in your right hand from the top, one by one, keeping them in the same order and count them aloud. Let the first card, the four of diamonds, protrude a quarter of an inch at the inner end, Fig. 1.

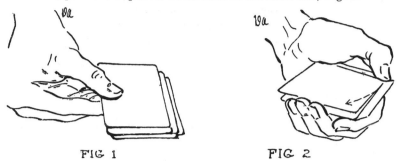

FIG. 1   FIG. 2

3.   Take the ninth card *on top* of the other counted cards and then put the packet of nine cards on top of the remainder of the pack in your left hand.

4.   Square the cards and with the right thumb make a break under the second card, the four of diamonds, its projecting end making this easy. Hold the break with the tip of the left second finger.

5.   Press the inner left corner of the pack firmly against the base of the left thumb and place the tip of the thumb on the outer left corner of the pack; push off the two cards, as one card, outwards and downwards, Fig. 2.

6.   Turn the right hand palm upwards, seize the two cards at the outer

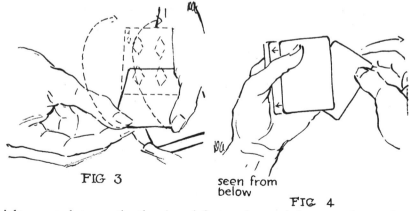

FIG. 3   seen from
                          below
                             FIG. 4

right corner between the thumb and first and second fingers and turn them over inwards, showing the four of diamonds, Fig. 3.

7. Retain the grip by the right thumb and first and second fingers and turn the cards over outwards, at the same time turning the left hand bringing its back upwards. Draw out the four of diamonds, face upwards and retain the indifferent card back of it flush with the pack with the left thumb, Fig. 4. Drop the four of diamonds face upwards on the table.

THE LYONS FORCE

L. Vosburgh Lyons, M.D.

Here is a method of forcing a card in which apparently, every possible precaution is taken to assure the spectator having a free choice, yet the force is made infallibly and with a minimum of trouble on the part of the performer. The method follows:

1. Invite a spectator to shuffle the pack, then put your hands behind your back, turn around and ask the spectator to put the cards, face downwards, in your hands.

2. Turn to face him, keeping your hands behind you, and quickly reverse the bottom card. To do this hold the pack by the ends between the thumb and fingers of the right hand, pull off the bottom card with the left fingers, turn it over by closing the left fingers, Fig. 1, and take the pack on top of it in that hand; at once bring the right hand forward.

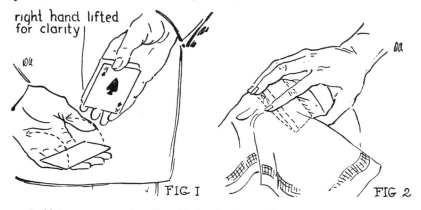

right hand lifted for clarity

FIG I   FIG 2

3. Take out your handkerchief, give it to the spectator asking him to spread it out and then throw it over your left hand and the pack. Turn around so that he can do this with the pack still behind you. Then turn to face him and bring the pack forward, still covered with the handkerchief.

4. With your right hand smooth the fabric over the pack and with the left fingers draw the upper end of the reversed card a little to the left, ex-

posing the top index. Tighten the fabric over this index with the right first and second fingers, the tip of the second finger pressing outwards and the tip of the first finger pressing inwards, Fig. 2. Read the index with a single glance, push the card flush with the pack with the left thumb and continue the action of smoothing the handkerchief over the pack. The sighting of the index takes place on the side of the deck away from the spectators and is, therefore, imperceptible to them.

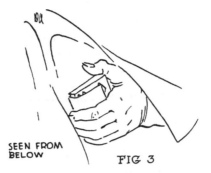

SEEN FROM
BELOW   FIG 3

5. With the left fingers push this sighted, reversed card off towards the right about half an inch and close the left fingers on it so that the right side of the card is bent against the side of the pack, Fig. 3.

6. Invite the spectator to cut the pack through the handkerchief and raise the pack several inches. With the cards in that position, give him the choice of taking more or fewer cards. When he is satisfied, push the reversed card upwards and over onto the lower part of the pack with the left fingers.

7. Have the spectator place his free hand underneath the handkerchief, with it push the top card of the lower half forward about half its length, and let the cut portion drop on top.

8. Instruct him to grip the protruding end of this card through the fabric with one hand and take the pack in the other.

So far as the spectator and the onlookers are concerned what has happened is this: He has made a free cut, pushed the card he cut at forward and he now holds that card with one hand and the pack with the other, both card and pack still being covered with the handkerchief.

9. As a still further guarantee of straightforwardness, you turn away while he withdraws the card from the pack, uncovers it and notes what card it is.

This force will be found specially useful in such feats as prediction tricks, in which it is necessary to persuade the spectators that a perfectly free choice of a card is given. For instance, having written a prediction, folded the paper and placed it on the table, you sight a card and force it as explained above. When you turn away while the spectator ascertains what card he has chosen, write its name, *Q. H.,* on a duplicate slip, fold it in the same way as the duplicate slip and finger palm it. Finally change the slips in apparently handing the original to another spectator to hold.

Another way would be to obtain a duplicate prepared slip from a pocket index.

DOUBLE LIFT SUBSTITUTE
DEANE MOORE

This sleight will be understood best by describing a trick in which it plays the leading role. We will assume that you wish to perform the Ambitious card effect, in which a card constantly returns to the top of the pack, without using the double lift.

1. After shuffling the pack, casually show the bottom card, say it is the four of diamonds. Place the pack in the left hand, square it and at the same time riffle off the ends of the two bottom cards with the right thumb. Hold a small break at that point with the tip of the left little finger.

2. Take the pack by the inner ends between the right thumb and the second finger and retain the break with the tip of the second finger.

3. Execute the Hindu shuffle, pulling off small packets from the top into the left hand until the break is reached, Fig. 1, and retain the last two cards as one. Hold the supposed single card up face outwards and ask the spectators to take particular notice of it, Fig. 2. Place it face downwards on the top of the pack.

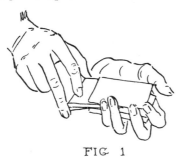

FIG 1

FIG 2

4.   Push off the top (indifferent) card with the left thumb and insert it in the middle of the deck.   After the usual hocus-pocus turn the top card and show that the four of diamonds has returned to the top of the pack.

5.   Turn the card face downwards and shuffle overhand, first lifting the whole of the pack except the top and bottom cards, retaining them in the left hand by pressure of the left thumb and fingers. Shuffle off the remainder of the deck on these cards.   Proceed to a couple of riffle shuffles retaining the two bottom cards in that position.

6.   Repeat the Hindu shuffle, as described above, until the two bottom cards are left alone in the right hand.   Lift the hand showing these two cards as one (the four of diamonds is behind the indifferent card).

7.   Place the two cards on the top of the pack, as one card, order the four of diamonds to return to the top, turn the top card and show it has obeyed you.

Other uses for the sleight will readily suggest themselves.

CARD CONTROL NO???

DEANE MOORE

1.   A card having been freely chosen, take it under pretence of seeing that it is placed fairly in the middle, and insert it somewhat below the middle of the squared deck, at the outer end.   Push it in until only about an inch of its end protrudes, Fig. 1.

2.   Press the tip of the left forefinger on the end of the packet below the protruding card.   Remark that you will push the card right through the deck and strike its protruding end with your right fingers, at the same moment push the lower packet with the left forefinger making it protrude an inch from the inner end of the pack.   The chosen card, therefore, remains at the bottom of the top portion, Fig. 2.

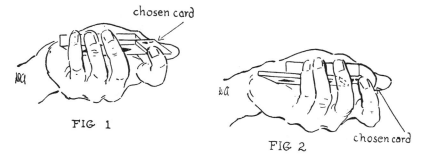

FIG 1   FIG 2

3. Draw away the protruding lower portion, keeping the packet perfectly squared, and place on the top as one card. Smartly done the action gives the illusion of the chosen card having been driven through the pack and then placed on top.

4. Remove the top card, an indifferent one, insert it in the pack and slowly push it flush with the other cards.

The chosen card is at the bottom of the pack, ready to be dealt with as the occasion demands.

It will be noted that this procedure makes a good follow-up for the preceding routine. This time you show your control of the card by making it pass to the bottom instead of the top.

THE CUT PASS

Frederick Braue

For best results the sleight should be executed at a medium pace, neither too fast nor too slow. Smoothly done the cuts appear to be without guile and the final result, the passage of the chosen card to the top of the pack is achieved without arousing any suspicion on the part of the spectator.

1. Hold the pack in the left hand as for dealing but with the first finger doubled underneath, its nail pressing against the face card. Retain a break with the left little finger at the right side above the card to be brought to the top.

2. Shift the pack so that it is held between the ball of the left thumb and the third phalanges of the second and third fingers, the fourth finger retaining the break as in figure 1.

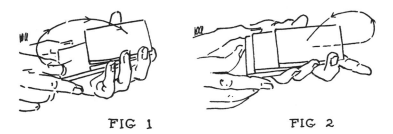

FIG 1   FIG 2

3. Strip out the lower half of the packet under the break by grasping it between the right thumb and second fingers, and drawing it off the inner end, Fig. 1. Place this packet on top of the pack but outjog it a quarter of an inch.

4. Remove all the remaining cards under the little finger break with the left hand and place them on top of the pack from the outer end and flush with the outjogged top packet. Fig. 2 shows the action of the left hand. For clarity, the outjog is greatly increased in the illustration.

5. Draw the original upper packet, those cards originally above the little finger break, inwards and place it on top, these cards being gripped between the right thumb and third finger during the action. In placing the packet on top, outjog it a quarter of an inch; thus the pack is divided by the outjogged upper packet into two parts.

6. Strip out half the lower packet with the left fingers and place this small packet upon the top, from the outer end, flush with that at the top of the pack.

7. Grip the remainder of the lower packet between the right thumb and third fingers and strip it inwards, placing it flush upon the remainder of the deck. The card originally under the little finger break at the middle of the pack is now at the top. Tap the pack on the table to square its sides and ends, thus tacitly proving that it is in honest condition. Figure 3 shows the sequence of the various cuts.

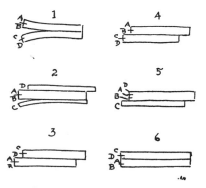

It is a good idea to finish with another false cut. Although any blind cut may be used, the following is well-suited to the needs:

Hold the pack in the left hand vertically on its side, the thumb and second, third and fourth fingers at the sides, the first finger at the outer end, and grasp the sides at the inner end between the thumb and second and third fingers of the right hand. Extend the right first finger rigidly outwards and press it against the top of the pack.

Strip out the *lower* half of the pack with the right hand, letting the wrist drop until the packet is clear, then bring the hand upwards towards the right and drop the packet onto the table.   At the same time move the left hand slightly towards the left and back.

Immediately grasp the packet remaining in the left hand and slap it down on that on the table.   Apparently a true cut has been made; actually it is a false cut, the desired card remaining at the top.

THE GROTE INSTANTANEOUS PALM
H. Walter Grote

Regarding this sleight, Mr. Grote writes as follows:

"I have used this sleight for years for the instantaneous palming of a top stock in such tricks as the *Cards to Pocket* and the *Thirty Cards Transposition*. Properly executed, without the least hesitation of the right hand, the sleight is invisible."

Here are the moves:

1.   Hold the pack in the left hand, face downwards, in the dealing position, the thumb on the side of the pack and the little finger tip inserted below the stock to be palmed, Fig. 1.

2.   In the action of pulling back the left sleeve, sweep the right hand across the left hand and, at the moment it reaches the right side of the deck, straighten out the left third and fourth fingers, thus lifting the stock into an upright position almost at a right angle with the deck, the left thumb acting as a stop, Fig. 2.

3.   Grip the cards in the right hand and carry them away without the least pause, continuing the sweep of the hand to the left sleeve and at once pulling it up a little.

4.   Drop the right hand to the side, or with it take the pack, which ever action is best suited to the trick being executed.

Practice before a mirror will make clear the exact timing required to make the steal indetectably.

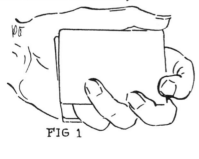

FIG 1

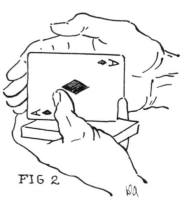

FIG 2

CHAPTER II.   FLOURISHES

THE DIP COLOR CHANGE

JOSEPH COTTONE

In this novel color change the face card of the deck is hidden momentarily by the width of the hand and not by its length as in other methods. The retention of a card in the covering hand seems to be out of the question, thereby strengthening the effect.

1.   Hold the pack in the left hand, upright, the bottom card facing the spectators, the thumb at one side, the fingers at the other, Fig. 1.

FIG 1

FIG 2

2.   Show the palm of the right hand as in figure 1, then turn it downwards so that it covers the upper half of the pack as in Fig. 2.

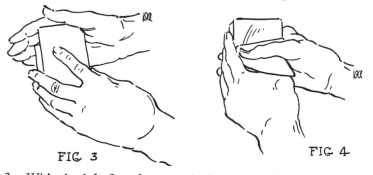

FIG 3

FIG 4

3.   With the left first finger push the rear card into the fork of the right thumb, hold it there and push the deck upwards with the left hand,

making it slide between the side of the first finger and the clipped card, until about half the length of the pack protrudes, Figs. 3, 4.

4.   Draw the pack upwards with the left hand, leaving the single card clipped by the right thumb and, at the same moment, tip the top of the right hand a little towards the audience.   The clipped card, extending at an angle from the thumb crotch, is hidden from the spectators although it lies across the hand, Fig. 5.

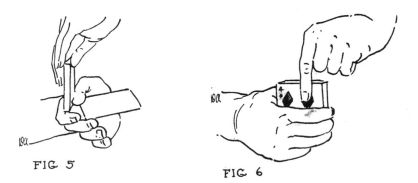

FIG 5

FIG 6

5.   Dip the pack into the right hand, placing it squarely on the clipped card, holding both together momentarily with the right thumb, then lift the pack upwards from the thumb crotch with the left thumb and forefinger, thus completing the color change, Fig. 6.

It is the upward movement of the pack in item 3 that makes the sleight so deceptive since there does not seem to be any possibility of the retention of a card in the right hand.

THE SNAP COLOR CHANGE

Joseph Cottone

This flourish is based on the Herrmann pass, a modification of the handling producing a very rapid and open color change and marking the first time the pass has been used for this purpose.

1.   Hold the pack in the left hand, vertically on its side, between the thumb above and the third joints of the second and third fingers below, the first and fourth fingers being free, Fig. 1.

2. Grip the lower corners of the pack with the right thumb at the inner corner, first and second fingers at the outer corner, bend the first and fourth left fingers behind the pack so that their nails rest against the back of the top, or rearmost, card, Fig. 2.

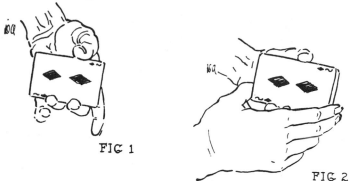

FIG 1

FIG 2

3. With the tips of the second and third left fingers pull back about half the pack, insert their top joints into the break and hold this rear packet firmly between the two fingers on its face and the curled first and fourth fingers at the back.

4. Swing the rear packet downwards to a horizontal position just below the lower side of the front packet in such a way that the front vertical half of the pack rests on the middle of the back of the horizontal half, Fig. 3. This movement of the rear half of the pack is covered by the front half,

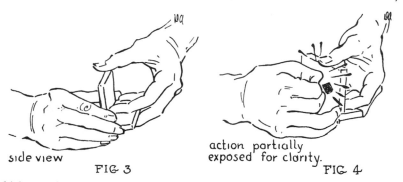

side view

FIG 3

action partially
exposed for clarity.

FIG 4

which remains stationary, and the back of the right hand. Release the front packet from the grip of the right thumb and fingers and support it on the back of the lower half by the left thumb only, on its upper side.

5.   Snap the face card with the right second finger, Fig. 4, press downwards with the left thumb and upwards with the left fingers, transposing the packets and bringing the face card of the original rear packet into view instantly.

When the right second finger is bent in against the tip of the thumb to make the snap, be careful to keep the right hand covering the lower part of the face card and the lower packet. The transposition of the two packets should be made in one instantaneous movement. At the completion of the change, raise the left hand a little and lower the right hand.

VISIBLE COLOR CHANGE

Joseph Cottone

1.   Hold the deck face outwards vertically on its side, between the right thumb and forefinger at the right lower index corner and the left thumb and forefinger at the upper index corner, the face card being jogged very slightly towards the right, Fig. 1   Curl the second, third and fourth fingers of each hand inwards.

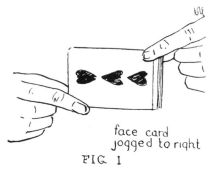

face card
jogged to right

FIG. 1

2.   Jerk the pack outwards quickly towards the spectators to a distance of about six inches, then back towards yourself. Under cover of this action, extend the right second finger, with it pull the face card to the rear of the deck and hold it there with the tips of this finger and the thumb, Figs. 2, 3. The stolen card should lie horizontally, with its inner end pointing towards the body.

3.   After the change hold the pack stationary for a few moments, then grasp it with the left hand, slide it into the right hand and square the cards, adding the stolen card to the top imperceptibly in the action.

Deftly performed the face card is flicked off so rapidly that its withdrawal cannot be perceived, the card simply changes visibly into another card.   In all these color changes it is advisable, where possible, to arrange that the two cards contrast markedly in color and value.

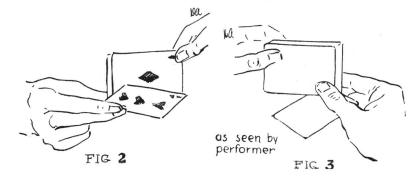

FIG 2

as seen by performer

FIG 3

CHAPTER III. TRICKS

THE MARRIAGE METER

FREDERICK BRAUE

EFFECT: Two spectators each select a card in a manner which is apparently determined by chance, yet both cards are identical in suit and value. The conjurer does not touch the cards at any time.

PREPARATION: With two packs of cards available, note the thirty-third card of one pack; let us say that this card is the act of hearts. Use the second pack for any other trick, at the end of which place its ace of hearts also thirty-third from the top. An easy way to do this is to bring the card to the bottom of the pack, thumb count ten cards at the top and cut them to the bottom; then thumb count nine more at the top and cut them also to the bottom.

METHOD: Choose for this feat a husband and wife, preferably a couple which obviously enjoys one another's company. Tell them that science can determine by laboratory experiment if any particular man is suited to any particular woman, and hence can determine beforehand if a marriage between such persons will be a success. Being a magician, you claim that you can dispense with cumbersome apparatus and secure the same information by using two packs of cards as a marriage-meter.

1. Hand one of the packs to the man, the other to the woman. Request each, acting in accord, to remove any card from the middle of the pack in hand and place it face downwards before the other. Have each person note the value of the card thus placed down and then deal on it, from the top of the deck, enough cards to bring the total to ten. Thus, if the man places a five spot before the woman, she is to deal five more cards upon it. Jacks, queens and kings are to be counted as tens in value. When one of them is dealt, no cards are placed upon it.

2. After this deal, request each person to place the top card of the pack in hand before the other, again have each note its value and deal upon it sufficient cards to bring the total to ten.

3. Have this procedure repeated with one more card.

4. Request each party to turn the three packets of cards thus made, face upwards and to add the values of the face cards. This, you explain, gives each person their number in the marriage-meter and you have them count down in the remainder of the pack in hand and remove the cards at their re-

spective numbers. You further explain that the particular card thus arrived at is the indicator card which reveals to each of them the marriage quotient.

5. Have the two cards thus discovered placed face downwards upon the table, one on the other and at right angles to it. After a few words in semi-serious vein about the infallibility of the test, have the two cards turned face upwards and show that they are identical—in this case, the ace of hearts. Offer this as proof that their marriage is a successful one and will remain so.

Under the required circumstances, namely the presence of an engaged couple, or a married couple, and particularly newly-weds, this self-working feat will be found highly effective.

DIOGENES' CARD

The cleverly disguised mathematical principle in the following trick makes it one of the best of self-working feats.

EFFECT: Two spectators each think of a card. The pack is shuffled and a card is chosen from it; this card *discovers* the two cards that were mentally selected.

FIG 1

FIG 2

METHOD: 1. Offer the pack for shuffling, take it back and deal cards in an overlapping row from right to left, silently counting them as you do so until you deal a card the value of which corresponds with the count. That is to say, if the fifth card is a five, remember this number; it is your key number. Fig. 1.

2. Continue to deal until ten or twelve cards are on the table. If it happens that there is no card in correct position for use as a key, you can generally fix for one by moving a card or two from one end of the line to the other by way of calling attention to the fact that it doesn't matter how the cards lie. Failing this, simply gather the cards and deal a fresh row. Having secured a key card, request one of the spectators to think of a num-

ber, and then to remember the card at that number as you tap each card in the row, beginning with the card on the extreme left. Do the same thing with a second spectator.

3. Gather the spread cards without changing their order and make a false shuffle, retaining the cards in their original order at the top of the pack. Undercut half the deck, injog the first card and shuffle off. Undercut at the injog and run one less than the key number, in this case four cards, and injog the card at the key number, in this case five. This action reverses the order of these five cards. Throw the remaining cards on top.

4. In squaring the cards, form a break above the injogged card and slip the tip of the left little finger into this break.

5. Force the key card under the break by any method you may prefer. As good a procedure as any is to riffle the outer end of the pack, request that *stop* be called at any point, and openly break the pack at the little finger break, no matter when *stop* may have been called (see the Riffle Force, p. 11). Remove the top card of the lower packet, the key card, and drop it face upwards on the table. In the present case it is a five.

6. Place the packet above the break to your right, the lower packet to the left, Fig. 2. Request the first spectator to tell you the number at which his original card lay in the original spread. Suppose he states that it was at *two*. Point to the key card and say "Deduct your number, two, from this freely selected value, five, and the remainder is three. Therefore we will remove three cards from this packet (the packet on the left) and the third card will be your card." Do this, and the spectator's mentally selected card is the last card turned, that is to say, at the count of three.

7. Ask the second spectator for the number of his card. It is, we will say, *eleven*. Point to the key card, a five, as we have supposed, and deduct five from eleven, leaving a remainder of six. Count down six cards in the right hand packet and the desired card will turn up on the last card.

If the instructions are followed accurately, the trick is entirely automatic, no matter what the value of the key card may be, or the numbers at which the spectators' cards may lie in the original spread. It is only necessary to remember that if the number at which a card lay is less than the value of the key card, it will be in the left hand packet; if it is larger, it will be in the right hand packet.

If both spectators have thought of a card at a number less than the value of the key card, it is necessary not to disarrange the order of the cards in dealing them from the left hand packet to find the first spectator's card, and to replace them in the same order on this packet before locating the second card. However, it is more striking to have each spectator's card appear in the separate packets. For this reason it is well to ask one spectator to remember one of the first few cards you deal and have the second spectator remember one of the last few cards.

THE TRIPLE DISCOVERY

CHARLES MILLER — JACK McMILLEN

This ingenious application of the principle of the **twenty-sixth** card location makes possible a triple discovery which gives **the** appearance of great skill, whereas the trick, in reality, is entirely self-**working**.

EFFECT: Three cards are chosen by three spectators **under** conditions which would seem to make their subsequent location by **the** conjurer wholly impossible. Nevertheless, they are produced in a **very striking** manner.

PREPARATION: Secretly daub the back of **any card**, or crimp its corner, and place this card twenty-sixth from the top of **the pack**.

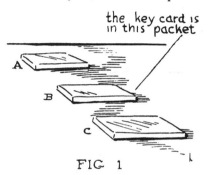

the key card is in this packet

FIG. 1

METHOD: 1. Secure a break under the marked **key card** and force this card upon spectator X. Have it replaced at the point from which it was taken and square the cards.

2. Make the following overhand shuffle: Shuffle off the first twenty cards freely and run the last ten one by one, after which shuffle off the remainder freely. This procedure changes the order of the cards near the top and bottom, but the key card moves one place only and is **now** the twenty-seventh card from the top. Repeat the shuffle and the key card will return to its original position, that is, twenty-sixth from the top.

3. Place the pack on the table and request a spectator **to cut** it into three packets A, B and C. The key card, X's card, **will be somewhere** in the middle packet, B, Fig. 1.

4.   Ask a second spectator, Y, to take packet C, shuffle it thoroughly and then note the card at its top.   Request a third spectator, Z, to take packet A, shuffle it, and to note the card at its face after the shuffle.

5.   Place A upon C and place both upon B.   Cut the pack several times, or have a spectator cut.

6.   Spread the cards face downwards from left to right in a long ribbon, find the marked key card and separate the spread at this point by pushing the cards to the left of the key card a little to one side.   Push forward the key card and request X to name his card.   Turn the marked key card face upwards, showing that it is his card.

7.   Reassemble the pack by placing all those cards to the left of the key card upon those to its right, the break in the spread making this an easy matter.   Do not replace the key card in the pack.   The cards chosen by Y and Z are now at twenty-six and twenty-seven from the top.

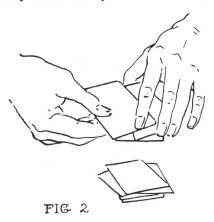

FIG. 2

8.   Hold the pack in the left hand and with the right fingers and thumb *milk* the pack by means of the Klondyke shuffle, Fig. 2; that is to say, draw a card from the top with the thumb as the fingers also draw off a card from the bottom, thus dropping the cards on the table in pairs.   When you have drawn off about six pairs in this way, in the next action draw but one card from the top of the deck, dropping it, and then continue *milking* the pack by drawing off the cards in pairs.

9.   Continue this procedure until only two cards remain in the left hand. Request spectators Y and Z to name their cards.   Turn the two cards remaining in the left hand and show that they are the cards named by the spectators.

CARD INSTINCT
Frederick Braue

Here is an ideal trick with which to begin a series of feats with cards. Its working is so fair and its successful culmination seems so impossible that the spectators are unconsciously made to feel that the performer can do anything he likes with the cards. This frame of mind makes succeeding feats so much the easier for him to accomplish.

EFFECT: 1. A spectator freely choses a card, he replaces it with the pack in his own hands and thoroughly shuffles the cards. The performer infallibly finds the chosen card and produces it in any way he desires.

PREPARATION: Beforehand remove the thirteen hearts from the pack and arrange them in order from the ace to the king, the ace being the first card. Place this stock at the top of the pack, Fig. 1, and put the pack in its case.

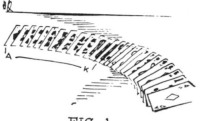

FIG 1

WORKING: Remove the cards from the case and execute a false shuffle, following this with several false cuts. Make a regular cut placing the heart stock in the middle so that the thirteen cards run approximately from twenty to thirty-three. Invite a spectator to take a card and run the cards from hand to hand so that one of the hearts is drawn. It should not be difficult to do this in such a way that the spectator will be convinced that he has had a perfectly free choice. Or, if you prefer it, spread the cards on the table and invite the spectator to remove a card. Almost infallibly, he will take a card from the middle part of the spread, thus getting one of the hearts.

2. Gather the cards and cut or pass the remaining twelve hearts to the top of the pack.

3. Square the pack and place it before the spectator. Request him to cut it at any place and return this card to the pack, and complete the cut. Ask him then to riffle shuffle the pack. When he has done that have him repeat the riffle shuffle. By the time he has done that he will be thoroughly satisfied that his card is lost in the deck.

4. Take the pack, run through the hearts which will be scattered throughout it but will still retain their sequence, with the exception of *the one card which was removed by the spectator.*

This principle of the double riffle shuffle with a set-up at the top of the pack is not new but it is still so little known that an explanation of the reason for it is in order here. The first riffle shuffle spreads the twelve hearts amongst the first twenty-six cards, still retaining their sequence. Even if, on the second riffle shuffle, the spectator cuts less than half the pack and the last two or three of the heart sequence are riffled amongst the top cards, they will still retain their order.

5. The chosen card will, therefore, be the single heart which is not in sequence. Thus, if in running through the pack from the top down, you find the ace, two, three, four and five of hearts, all running in regular order although separated by indifferent cards, and the next heart, after the five is the seven, then the six of hearts is the chosen card.

Armed with this knowledge you can reveal the card in any way that you wish.

THE CHALLENGER

FREDERICK BRAUE

This very ingenious method for the discovery of a card which is, apparently, irrecoverably lost in the pack, also depends upon a set-up. However, the system is so simple that it can be made under the very noses of the spectators without creating any suspicion.

While toying with the pack, sort the bottom twelve cards so that they run red, black, red, black, alternately. Do the same with the first twelve cards of the pack so that they, too, are alternately red and black. If the bottom card of the pack is a black one, the top card must be a red one and vice versa. The operator will be surprised how often, in making this alternate color set-up, the movement of as few as three cards will establish the arrangement. Fig. 1.

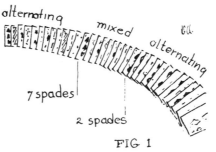

FIG 1

Note the bottom card, say it is the two of spades, and also the last card of the set-up at the top, which we will suppose is the seven of spades. Remember these two cards. If you cut the pack to bring the twenty-four cards to the middle, the cards between the two of spades and the seven of spades will be the cards set-up alternately red and black.

WORKING: Take the pack and fan it to show that the cards are apparently in a haphazard order; the red-black arrangement at the top and bottom will never be noticed by the keenest observer. Spread the cards ribbonwise on the table and invite a spectator to choose a card. Almost infallibly he will take one from the twenty-eight cards in the middle of the spread.

Gather the cards and cut the pack to bring the set-up cards to the middle. Square the pack, place it on the table and invite the spectator to cut and replace his card, putting the cut on top and then squaring the pack.

The cut will be made somewhere near the middle so that the chosen card will be replaced amongst the cards of the alternate-color set-up.

Take the pack and make an overhand shuffle as follows: Run about ten cards from the top and throw the remainder on top of these. Undercut about twenty cards and shuffle them onto the top. This procedure will retain the set-up cards intact.

Fan the cards with their faces towards you. You will find either two black cards or two red cards together in the set-up. Cut to bring one of them to the top, the other to the bottom. In looking for the two cards, the key cards you noted at first, in this case the two and the seven of spades, act as your guides. You do not know which of the two cards is the chosen card but you do know that one of them is the card you want. An assertion that you make and the spectator's reaction to it, or his reply to a leading question that you put to him, will solve this difficulty for you.

Finish the trick by revealing the card in the most striking way you can devise.

In the case where a perverse spectator, when originally selecting a card, takes one from amongst the set-up cards proceed in just the same way as explained above. You will then find two pairs of cards of the same color and you will, therefore, know that the wanted card is one of the four. However, if the ribbon spread is made in a semi-circular fashion with the apex towards the spectator, it will rarely happen that a card is taken from anywhere but the middle section. Further, completion of the trick leaves you ready for a repetition if desired; merely bury the extra card amongst those which are not in the alternate set-up section.

A trial of this ingenious trick will surely result in its addition to your repertoire.

ACES UP

Bert Allerton

This little feat, when introduced as an impromptu effect between other tricks, makes a pleasant interlude and gives the impression of great dexterity.

EFFECT: A red ace and a black one, placed fairly in the middle of the pack, jump to the top and the bottom.

PREPARATION: Place the ace of hearts at the top of the pack and the ace of spades at the bottom. Bridge the upper half of the pack downwards, the lower half upwards. To do this, first bend the entire deck upwards, then cut off about half the cards and bend these downwards by springing them onto the cards in the left hand. Fig. 2.

BEFORE THE FIRST CHARLIER PASS.   AFTER THE PASS.

FIG 2

FIG 1

METHOD: 1. Show the bottom card, the spade ace and also the top card, the heart ace, calling their names.

2. Hold the pack in the left hand by its sides in preparation for the Charlier pass and remove the black ace with the right hand. As you hold it up to display it, make the Charlier pass at the bridge, the left thumb preventing the packets from closing upon completion of the pass, Fig. 1. Place the black ace in this break, thus bringing it above the ace of hearts, and square the pack.

3. Remove the top card of the pack, calling it the ace of hearts without showing its face; actually, it is an indifferent card. Openly make another Charlier pass, the pack breaking open at the bridge. After the packets have been transposed, hold them apart, as in the previous action, with the left thumb, and drop the card in your right hand between them. Square the pack.

4. Show that the black ace is again at the bottom and the red ace at the top.

This method of performing a familiar trick depends for its effectiveness on the fact that the onlookers do not follow the position of the aces during the shifting of the packets and their ignorance of the conjurer's ability to make the pass at the bridge.

BIRDS OF A FEATHER

R. W. JAMISON

Mr. Jamison says, "This trick is a fast, snappy demonstration of the truth of the title, but is usually dubbed a four ace trick. The whole routine requires only about a minute."

EFFECT: Four packets of four cards each having been dealt with an ace at the bottom of each packet, the four aces assemble in one pile. Then the four queens are shown, one is placed in the performer's pocket, the other three in the pack. At command the three queens leave the pack and all four are produced from the pocket.

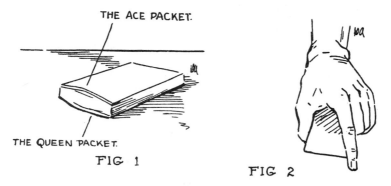

THE ACE PACKET.

THE QUEEN PACKET.

FIG 1

FIG 2

PREPARATION: A simple set-up is necessary. On the top of the pack arrange two aces, then three indifferent cards followed by the remaining two aces and on the face of the deck have two queens, three indifferent cards behind them and behind these the other two queens. Bridge the inner ends of the two packets of seven cards each, so that you can remove them easily, Fig. 1.

PRESENTATION: *First Phase:*

1. Lift off the top seven cards, saying that you will use the four aces. Hold the packet in the left hand as for the Repeat Count, Fig. 2. Show the ace at the face, drop the hand and glide the bottom card back.

2. With the right thumb above, fingers below, draw off the top card, showing it and counting *one*. Draw off the second ace on top of the first,

overlapping it a little so that the index is visible, and count *two*. Draw off the third ace and the three cards behind it, as one card, overlapping the second ace a little, counting *three* and at once snap the last ace in the left hand and count *four*.

3. Place the last ace on top of the cards in the right hand, square the packet and place it on top of the pack.

4. Deal the top card face downwards on the table, allowing a flash of its face. Deal the next three cards, the three indifferent cards, face downwards in a row. On the first card, an ace, deal the next three cards (aces), then deal three indifferent cards on each of the other three supposed aces.

5. Do not waste time forcing a packet, simply announce that you will use one packet and push the ace packet to one side. Gather the other packets with a sweep and place the cards on top of the pack.

6. Riffle the pack loudly and say *Go*. Let a spectator turn the packet on the table, revealing the four aces.

Second phase:

1. Take advantage of this surprise to remove the four queens packet from the face of the deck, slide the face queen down about a quarter of an inch and hold the packet near the bottom, face outwards, in the left hand between the thumb on one side, the fingers on the other side.

2. With the tip of the right forefinger pull back the top of the queen at the rear of the packet, grip it with the thumb, pull it out and show its face, naming it. Grip the inner end of the card between the tips of the right second and third fingers and retain it in that position.

3. Pull back the upper end of the second queen. Pull it out in the same way as you did the first one, name it and take it between the tips of the first and second fingers. Pull back the upper end of the packet of four cards, the dropping of the face queen enables you to do this easily and cleanly, draw out the packet as *one card*, naming the queen on its face and

FIG 3

hold the packet between the tips of the thumb and first fingers, Fig. 3. At once snap the fourth queen in the left hand and call its name.

4. Place this last queen on the face of the cards in the right hand and square the packet. This method of handling is very convincing.

5. Hold the packet in the left hand face downwards between the tips of the thumb and fingers on the sides, the tip of the forefinger at the outer end, and this end of the packet pointing downwards a little to hide the extra thickness. With the right thumb lift the top card as if it were hinged at the outer end, thus keeping its back to the front and place it on the top of the pack. Do the same with the next two cards, thus placing all three indifferent cards on the top of the pack.

6. Take the remaining four cards, the queens, as *one card,* between the right thumb at the outer end and the fingers at the inner end, saying, "And this last queen I will place in my pocket." Do so.

7. Cut the pack, riffle the ends loudly, and then spread the cards face upwards on the table with a wide sweep, as you say, "No queens here. Being birds of a feather they have come together in my pocket." Remove the four queens from your pocket, showing them and counting, "one, two, three, four."

These two tricks are routined specially for club performances in which it is necessary to stick strictly to essentials, wasting no time in arriving at your climax. Worked smartly they will be found very effective.

THE CARDS RISE AGAIN

R. M. JAMISON

Mr. Jamison says, "Magicians have for years endeavored to discover a perfect card rising routine, but there never was nor ever will be one that will suit every working condition or the predilections of every worker. So for years, after trying out every new rising card idea, I have finally devised the following method which is just as effective as the most intricate routine. One striking point is that it is self-contained, is always ready, has no difficult forcing nor shuffling, and you do not need a table, which makes it ideal for the usual club work. Although the inevitable thread is in use, it is a short one and cannot get tangled at the wrong time, nor do you have to hunt for it when it is needed."

PREPARATION: Two cards only rise in this method, we will suppose that they are the jack of diamonds and the ten of clubs. To prepare the *riser packet,* take two indifferent cards and punch a small hole in each near one end. Tie a knot in the end of a fine black silk thread, pass the knot through the holes in the two cards, from back to front, and engage it in a slit in the end of a third card, the knot coming directly opposite to the holes in the two threaded cards.   Push the jack of diamonds down between the face card of the packet of three, so that it carries the thread down with it.   Next push the ten of clubs down between the two punched cards in the same way. Cut the thread, leaving the free end a little longer than the length of a card and attach it to the bottom of the joker, Fig. 1.   Place this packet on the face of the deck, the two cards to be forced on the top and the whole pack in the houlette, Fig. 2.   Everything is ready.

FIG. 1   FIG. 2

PRESENTATION: 1.   Pick up the houlette, remove the pack and hand the houlette to a spectator for examination.

2.   Cut the squared-up pack at about the middle, slipping the top card to the lower half and hold half the pack in each hand.   Thus you have a force card on top of each packet and you simply thumb these cards off to spectators, one on each side of you.   This force is a Larsen-Wright idea and is known as the *Nerve force*.

3.   Have the two selected cards pushed into the squared up pack in different places and again square the cards.   Do this so fairly and openly that the spectators must be convinced that the cards are really lost amongst the other cards, making a shuffle entirely superfluous.   Pull the joker upwards about half an inch and make one cut, taking it and the riser packet to the middle.

4.   Take back the houlette.   Place the pack in it and hold the houlette in your left hand.   Have the first card that is to rise named, in this case it is the ten of clubs, and with your right hand take out the joker, gripping its lower end.   Keep your hand down near the top of the houllete and gently fan the pack with the joker, pulling the thread gradually, and the first card rises.

5.   When the card has risen almost to its full length, hold the joker behind it flat on the top of the houlette, hiding the thread and invite the spectator to remove his card himself.

6. Have the second card named and make it rise in exactly the same way. As the second spectator removes his card, give the joker a twist to take up the slack of the thread and thrust it into the deck. Place houlette and deck aside and go into your next trick.

Mr. Jamison says, "There is positively no reason whatever for giving out the deck; the houlette has already been examined. Further there is no need to worry about the threaded packet being disarranged when cutting the pack, it won't and the cards rise from the center of the deck, another strong point."

TRIPLE PREDICTION

EFFECT: The magician writes a prediction which proves to have accurately foretold the number of cigarettes in a borrowed package, the name of a card and the number at which it is found reversed in a shuffled pack, which has been wrapped in a pocket handkerchief and held by a spectator.

REQUIREMENTS: Any pack of cards, a small note book (two for 5c at the dime stores) and a pencil stub in the right coat pocket.

WORKING: 1. Have the deck shuffled by a spectator, turn round and receive it behind your back. Keeping your hands behind your back, put the pack in your left hand, turn to face the spectator and palm the top card in your right hand.

2. Bring your right hand forward, take your handkerchief from your outer breast pocket and give it to a spectator, at the same time sight the palmed card. Ask the spectator to spread the handkerchief and, as he does so, place your right hand behind your back and slip the palmed card to the bottom of the deck, reversed. Hold the pack in your left hand.

3. Turn away from the spectator again and have him spread the handkerchief over your left hand and the pack. This done, turn to face him and, still holding the cards behind you, turn the deck over underneath the handkerchief, bringing the reversed card uppermost. With your left thumb riffle off five cards and hold the break at that point.

4. Ask for an opened packet of cigarettes and have the owner spill the contents onto the table. In the meantime casually place your right hand in your coat pocket and with the pencil stub write on the first page of the note book the name of the sighted card, the seven of hearts, for example. (It suffices to write 7H.) If there are only a few cigarettes in the packet, one glance will give you the number. At once look away as you ask the spectator to count them; write the number under the name of the card, close the booklet, bring it out and toss it onto the table, without making any remark about it.

5. With the left hand riffle off cards to make up the number of cigarettes, make the Charlier pass at that point and bring the left hand forward with the pack still covered by the handkerchief. Wrap the fabric around the pack and give the bundle to a spectator to hold.

6. The mechanical part of the trick is complete, it only remains to build up the effect somewhat after this style: "I had a curious dream last night but when I awoke this morning all I could recall was a number and a card. However, the impression was so vivid that I at once wrote both in my notebook. Now we have arrived at a number purely by chance. How many cigarettes are there? Eight? Will you unwrap the pack and count down to that number? You find the eighth card reversed and it is the seven of hearts?"

Addressing another spectator, you continue, "Will you open my notebook and read out the name of the card and the number I wrote there this morning? Seven of hearts and number 8. Strange indeed; how can one account for such things."

If there are too many cigarettes to count at a glance, you can easily get the total number before the spectator finishes counting, then turn your gaze away and proceed as above.

In the unlikely chance that a packet of cigarettes is not available, have someone drop a handful of loose change on the table and use the number of coins.

AUTO-LOCATION

Joseph Cottone

Here is a very pretty quick trick suitable for introduction at any point in a card routine.

EFFECT: A spectator having selected a card, it is replaced and the pack is shuffled. The spectator takes the pack in his own hands and by a perfectly free riffle, he locates the very card he chose.

METHOD: 1. Using any pack, begin by having a card freely selected by a spectator, have it replaced and bring it to the top, using anyone of the various methods you may have at your command. Execute a false shuffle and a false cut, leaving the card on the top of the pack.

2. Show that the selected card is not on the bottom, then make a double lift and show that it is not on the top either. We will suppose that the top card, the card chosen, is the ace of spades, while the second card, the one shown by the double lift, is the two of diamonds. Turn the two cards face

downwards and take them, *as one card,* by the inner ends in your right hand, the thumb on top and the fingers below.   Hand the pack to the spectator.

3.   Invite him to riffle the outer ends of the cards, face downwards, and to stop at any point he pleases.   When he has done this, insert the two cards you hold, *as one card,* retaining your hold, Fig. 1, and instruct the spectator to release the riffled cards letting them fall on top.

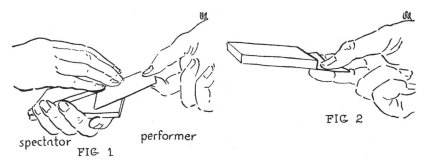

spectator   performer
FIG. 1   FIG 2

4.   Withdraw the double-lift cards with the spectator's cut balanced on top of them, Fig. 2.   Have the spectator turn his right hand palm upwards and ask him to name the card he chose.   The moment he replies, in this case, "Ace of spades," turn the balanced packet over onto his palm, face upwards, at the same moment pushing the ace of spades forward with your thumb and leaving it face upwards on the face of the packet on his hand,

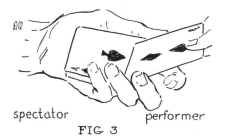

spectator   performer
FIG 3

Fig. 3, withdrawing the two of diamonds which alone remains in your right hand between the tips of your thumb and fingers.

The action is easy, but completely deceptive.   To all appearances, the spectator has actually cut the pack at his own card.   The trick makes a valuable addition to the list of effective impromptu feats which can be done under any circumstances, even when surrounded by spectators.

THE AERIAL COUNT
Joseph Cottone

EFFECT: A card having been chosen by a spectator, returned and the pack shuffled, the spectator names a number. The performer throws the cards, one by one, from his left hand into his right, beginning with the top card, and the chosen card appears at the number called.

METHOD: 1. Using any pack allow a spectator to choose any card he pleases, note it and return it to the pack. Control the card to the top by any method you prefer, shuffle the cards overhand to bring the card to the bottom, then make several cuts, leaving it in that position.

2. Invite the spectator to name any number between, say, one and twelve, "Merely," you remark, "in order not to make the operation too long."

3. Hold the pack in the left hand, face downwards, with the first and second fingers lying along the upper end, the third and fourth fingers underneath as shown in the figures. Place your right hand at a distance of about seven inches from the left hand and slightly lower than it. Push off the top card with the left thumb, and with a swing of the hand towards the right, throw it so that it lands face downwards on the palm of the right hand, counting *one*, Fig. 1. Turn the right hand over and slap this card down onto the table, face upwards, Fig. 2.

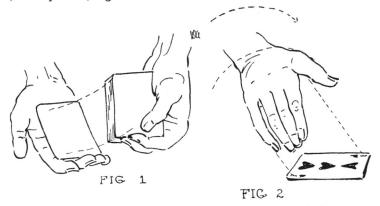

FIG 1   FIG 2

4. Continue throwing the cards one by one into the right hand, counting and slapping them down onto the table in this manner until the number called for is reached. Then, in the action of swinging the left hand towards the right, push the top card partly off the pack with the left thumb and, at the same moment, push out the bottom card with the third and fourth fingers, release it and throw it onto the right hand, at once pulling the top card back flush with the remainder of the deck, Fig. 3.

5. Hold out the right hand with the card lying face downwards upon it, have the selected card named and slap it, face upwards, on the other cards lying on the table.

A little practice is required to throw out the bottom card cleanly, synchronizing the throw with the pushing out and pulling back of the top card, but deftly performed the illusion is perfect. This method makes a very effective variation of the favorite plot of producing a chosen card at any number in the deck.

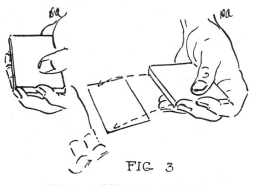

FIG. 3

THE JUMPING JOKER
JOSEPH COTTONE

EFFECT: A card is selected, replaced and the pack shuffled. The performer places his right hand over the deck and the selected card instantly flies out of the deck onto the table.

METHOD: 1. Following the usual processes, a card is selected by a spectator, replaced and controlled to the top. By means of an overhand shuffle, bring the chosen card to the bottom, then make several riffle shuffles and false cuts, retaining it in that position.

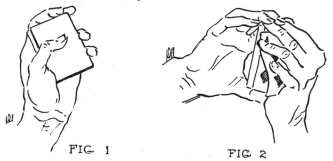

FIG. 1   FIG. 2

2. Hold the pack in the left hand by pressure of the top joint of the second finger on the outer right corner, the opposite diagonal corner being thus held firmly against the base of the thumb, the forefinger resting against the outer end and the third and fourth fingers against the right side of the pack, but taking no part in its actual maintenance, Fig. 1.

3. Bring the right hand over and, as soon as it covers the deck, pull back the bottom card with the tip of the left third finger, Fig. 2, release the card quickly, making it fly from the pack onto the table, Fig. 3.

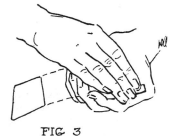

FIG 3

There must be no movement of the left hand which must remain stationary as the right hand covers it. In performing this effective little quick trick, Mr. Cottone forces the joker, hence the name he has given to it.

The reader should refer to the article *To shuffle or not to shuffle* on page 9. In this case it is palpable that the effect is much greater if the pack is squared immediately on the return of the chosen card than if a shuffle is executed.

MAGNETIC THOUGHT

BERT ALLERTON

The following feat is another of those in the working repertoire of Mr. Bert Allerton, whose table work at exclusive West Coast hotels has gained him an enviable reputation. That it is effective is proven by the fact that, using only the strongest audience tricks, Mr. Allerton has included this feat in his performances for many years.

EFFECT: Two cards are placed face downwards upon the table, the magician promising to place his hand upon whichever of the two may be thought of by a spectator. He succeeds in his attempts several times until at last he apparently fails, since he places his hand upon the wrong card. Nothing daunted, he flips this wrong card face upwards and shows that it has been magically transformed into the card of which the spectator is thinking.

METHOD: Hold the pack in the left hand as for dealing and with the thumb push the two top cards to the right, making them overlap, Fig. 1. Press the tip of the second finger upwards firmly against the face of the second card.

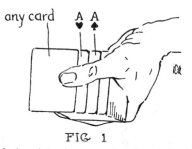

any card   A A
            ♥ ♠

FIG. 1

2. Turn the left hand back upwards, thus bringing the pack face upwards, at the same time bending the thumb inwards and with its tip draw the top card inwards, towards the left. The pressure of the second finger tip upon the face of the second card prevents its being drawn back during this action. Thus, when the hand is turned over, the second card, behind which the top card is hidden, will be seen protruding from the pack and will be taken for the top card, Fig. 2. Moreover, the index of the third card (supposedly the second card) can also be seen and this latter affords apparent proof that the card being shown is actually placed on the table. We will suppose this third card is the ace of hearts.

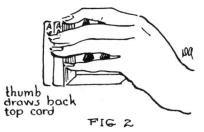

thumb
draws back
top card

FIG. 2

Call the attention of the spectators to the card you are showing, and name it aloud. Let us say it is the ace of spades.

3. Turn the hand back upwards, bringing the back of the pack uppermost, and push the top card out with the thumb, at the same moment causing it to extend beyond the second card. Drop this indifferent card upon the table, to your left, calling it the ace of spades.

4. Repeat the actions in items 1 and 2. The card you now show as the top card is the original, third card, the ace of hearts. Name it and apparently

place it face downwards to your right, actually you repeat the action in item 3 and thus place the ace of spades at your right.

5. Call attention to the fact that the ace of spades is the card to your left and the ace of hearts is the card to your right. Actually, an indifferent card is on your left, while the ace of spades is on your right.

Request a spectator to think of either of the cards and claim that infallibly, by a magnetic attraction, your hand will be drawn to the card of which he thinks. Hold your right hand above the two cards, and slowly, as though obeying an instinct place it upon the card at your right. Ask the spectator to name the card of which he is thinking. If he names the heart ace (the card supposed to be on your right) you have apparently succeeded in placing your hand upon the proper card. Pick up the two cards, without showing their faces, and drop them upon the pack, cutting it to bury the cards.

6. Repeat the trick until apparently you have failed. The procedure then is this: You have placed your hand upon the card to the right which the spectator believes to be the ace of hearts. He states that he thought of the ace of spades. "I knew you would think of that card," you say, "and to prove to you that I have actually read your mind, here is the ace of spades."

Turn over the card at your right and show that it is the ace of spades.

This feat is a fine one for close-up intimate work and is used by Mr. Allerton with great success. The unexpected transposition of the cards, turning what has seemed to be a failure, into a success, makes the trick one of the best of the surprise-ending feats. It will be noted that the top change used in this feat is performed with one hand only.

A DOUBLE-DYED SWINDLE

In this series the use of prepared cards has been omitted, with the exception of double-faced cards. Such cards can be introduced into a borrowed deck, they can be shown and handled freely so long as one face only is exposed and they lend themselves to many startling feats which are not possible otherwise. Here is one as done by Fred Rothenberg.

EFFECT: A spectator freely choses a card from a borrowed deck, notes it and replaces it fairly in the middle. The performer orders that card to reverse itself and, on spreading the cards, one of them is found to be faced but it is not the spectator's card. However, by merely having the spectator place his hand upon the pack for a moment, his card rises to the top from which he takes it himself. Then the card that was first found vanishes from the pack and is found in the performer's pocket.

PREPARATION: A double-faced card, say queen of hearts-nine of spades, is required; place this card in a handy pocket from which you can palm it with the nine of spades face outwards. Seize any favorable opportunity to remove the regular nine of spades from the pack you are working with and place it in your right trouser pocket. Secretly add the double-faced card to the bottom of the pack, making the queen side the face card of the deck. Then:

1. Shuffle freely, but retain the double-faced card at the bottom, and have a card freely selected by a spectator. Undercut for its return, thus bringing the double-faced card on top of it.

2. Square the pack meticulously, holding it as openly as possible, and do not make any such remark as this, "You see I do not make the pass," and so on. Simply make it obvious that no manipulation takes place.

3. Announce that you will make the chosen card turn face upwards in the pack. Riffle the pack lightly, run through the cards, one by one, face downwards, passing them from the left hand to the right until you come to the nine of spades side of the double-faced card. Show it and claim that you have succeeded in your undertaking.

4. The spectator disclaims that card and you are momentarily embarrassed and humiliated. Then recall that the nine of spades is the most mischievous card in the pack, always pushing itself forward, and while talking, take the double-faced card below the cards in your right hand and separate your hands a little. The chosen card is now the top card of the packet in your left hand.

5. Put the two packets together with the left hand packet above the one in your right hand. Ask the spectator to put his hand on top of the pack which you hold face down in your right hand. Riffle the bottom cards with your left little finger and ask him if he felt anything. He replies *yes*. "That was your card rising to the top," you say. Have him name his card and turn it face upwards himself.

6. Remark that you will deal with that mischievous nine of spades, turn the pack face upwards and run through it looking for the card. It has vanished; you search your pockets and finally produce the regular nine of spades from your right trouser pocket. Under cover of this surprise it is an easy matter to palm the double-faced card from the bottom of the pack in your left hand and pocket it.

The trick is effective and it is a curious fact that whereas the wrong card is shown reversed in the deck, nobody ever remarks on the fact that you search for it with the pack face upwards.

THE DIMINISHING CARDS

Sleight of Hand Method

One of the prettiest of card tricks, this feat of successively diminishing the size of a pack of cards was created by Robert-Houdin and, curiously enough, the method of making the various fans which the great Frenchman employed is still the best. Unfortunately, the modern conjurer has almost universally abandoned the Houdin thumb-spread method in favor of that in which the fan is made by pressure. This latter method is wholly unsuited to the trick, since of necessity the onlookers perceive the entire pack as the conjurer adjusts it for each successive fan, the illusion of the feat being destroyed thereby.

Two factors have contributed to the neglect of the Houdin method. One is that although Houdin explained *how* the trick was performed, he did not explain in detail the nature of the various actions, leaving each reader to discover these for himself. A second is that, although his *Secrets of Conjuring and Magic* is one of the great textbooks, it has not been widely read by the conjurers of this country.

The following modern routine makes of the Diminishing Cards one of the most ingratiating feats in the realm of conjuring.

EFFECT: A pack of cards is fanned in a half circle; it is closed and, upon being again fanned, proves to be greatly diminished in size. This is repeated once more, when the pack is seen to be very small indeed; and when it is fanned for the last time, it is seen to have vanished entirely.

REQUIREMENTS: A pack of thirty-two cards, which may or may not been treated with corn starch or zinc stearate to ensure easier fanning, as the individual performer may decide for himself; place the ace of diamonds at the face of the pack. Also a small tray, so placed that it extends partly over the inner end of the conjurer's table, which should be on his left.

METHOD: The trick may be used either as a finale to a card fanning routine or as a pseudo-explanation of *The Cards to the Pocket,* the latter being the use to which Robert-Houdin put the feat. In either case, the conjurer explains what he purposes to do, declaring that the cards can be caused to diminish at will.

Begin by squaring the pack and then place it in the left hand in position for making the pressure fan. (*) Do not bevel the sides of the pack;

(*) Expert Card Technique, page 164.

although this makes the pressure fan easier of accomplishment it reduces the size of the fan.

Make a pressure fan in the following manner: As the right hand moves the cards to the right, allow them also to slide along the length of the left first finger until the cards are spread upon this finger to its tip. Complete the fan in the usual manner. The resultant fan is not circular, but oval, the cards at the hub forming an elongated horseshoe, Fig. 1. A fan thus made shows the maximum of the faces of the cards.

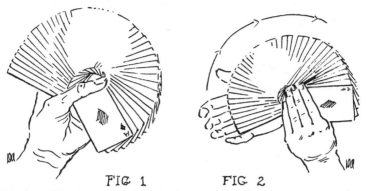

FIG 1   FIG 2

Display this fan and close it by pressing its lower corner into the crotch of the right little finger, the palm of this hand being in a vertical position facing the left, Fig. 2. Close the fan by bringing the right hand upwards and then to the left. Thus, when the fan is closed, the fingers of the right hand rest upon the outer end of the deck, concealing it, and the right

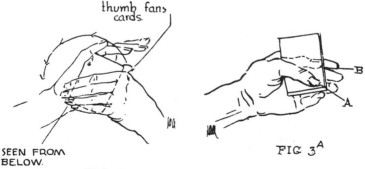

thumb fans
cards.

SEEN FROM
BELOW.

FIG 3   FIG 3^A

FIG 3^A

thumb rests on the left side at the outer corner in the proper position to make a fan by the thumb-spread method, Fig. 3. The pack itself, resting upon the left palm, is hidden by the back of this hand.

Note that in this position the tip of the left third finger presses upon the lower right corner. Move the left thumb at the back of the pack so that its ball rests upon the same corner, as in Fig. 3A at A. Spread the pack in a half-circle by moving the right hand in the same action as that used in the pressure fan, but actually spread the cards with the ball of the right thumb, Fig. 3. At the completion of the fanning movement, the pack appears to be greatly reduced in size, Fig. 4.

Display this fan and close it as previously described; at the completion of this action the pack will again be as in Fig. 3.

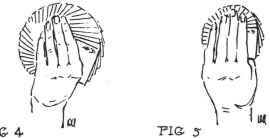

FIG 4   FIG 5

Shift the left thumb and place its tip upon the cards at B, Fig. 3-A, and again fan the cards, using the right thumb to spread them. They fan into a complete circle (this fan is known as the Rosette) and so little of the outer ends appears beyond the finger tips that the pack appears to have been reduced to the size of a set of midget cards, Fig. 5.

It should be noted that when the pack is gripped as outlined above, there is no necessity to shift it in the left hand; all that must be done is to move the left thumb. Thus the full faces of the cards are never exposed to the view of the audience, a fault which destroys the illusion of diminishment.

Display this fan and close it, using the method described above. Immediately the fan is closed, palm the pack in the right hand in this manner: Press down upon the outer end, at the same moment removing the left thumb. The pack is thus levered up against the side of the left forefinger into the right palm, Fig. 6. Place the tip of the left thumb against the tips of the left fingers and as soon as the right hand tightens upon the pack in its palm, move it downwards to the right in an action which exactly simulates that previously used in fanning the cards, Fig. 6. Hold the left hand with its fingers in a vertical position, the thumb pressed against the fingers as though holding a very small pack.

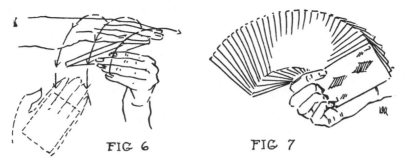

FIG. 6   FIG. 7

Retaining the pack, palmed in your right hand, pick up the tray from the table at your left, thus covering the palmed cards, and with the left fingers apparently sprinkle the cards upon it, explaining that they are now so small that they are invisible.

It is a good idea to have a silk handkerchief upon the table so that when the tray is placed on it and the cards are released, the slanting elevation of the tray will not seem to be suspicious.

This routine, a very pretty one to watch, is a favorite of Mr. Charles Miller's and, in his hands, it creates a perfect illusion.

A very clever subtlety is made use of in the routine for this trick as performed by Mr. Paul LePaul, to whom the magic fraternity is indebted for many good things. (*)

The trick is performed exactly as described above save that immediately prior to its execution, approximately twenty cards are removed from a complete deck of fifty-two and dropped face downwards upon a table, which is at the conjurer's right.

Then, as you display each fan in the left hand, drop the right hand upon the packet of twenty resting on the table, and placing the fingers upon the outer ends, pick up these cards by drawing the hands inwards. Thus, when the cards are removed from the table they are in the proper position to be gripped with the first and little fingers at the sides, the second and third fingers at the ends, in position for the one hand fan. Make such a fan, Fig. 7, and as each of the progressively smaller fans is shown, compare the fan in the right hand with that in the left, as if merely to show the difference in

(*) In "Expert Card Technique" by Jean Hugard and Fred Braue, a novelty card discovery originated by Mr. LePaul was included under the title of "There It Is." Unaware at that time of the origin of the feat, this belated acknowledgment is made to Mr. LePaul.

size. After each such comparison drop the right hand fan face downwards upon the table, squaring the cards.

In the final action of the trick, in which the pack is caused to vanish from the left hand, drop the right hand *with the palmed cards* upon the twenty cards resting face downwards on the table and at once pick up the entire pack and again make a one hand fan, the palmed cards being added to the smaller packet in the action. With the fan made with the combined packets, fan the left hand; open this hand and show that the cards have vanished.

This clever stratagem, by the use of which the conjurer can get rid of the palmed cards, will be found practical and extremely deceptive. It is a better method than the use of a tray to cover the palmed cards.

THE DIMINISHING CARDS

Mechanical Method

CHARLES MILLER

This method of performing the classic trick is notable for its simplicity and ease of execution.

EFFECT: A pack of cards diminishes by degrees and finally disappears into thin air.

REQUIREMENTS: Two packs of Bee playing cards, or any similar brand with a striped all-over back pattern; a pack of half-size cards and a pack of quarter-size cards. To make these smaller cards, split forty full size cards, twenty of the half-size cards and also twenty of the quarter-size. With rubber cement attach the faces of the smaller cards to the backs of the full-size cards and trim off the extra width and length. Thus you will have cards of three different sizes with backs to match.

PREPARATION: Place twenty of the full-size cards face downwards on the table. Upon these place twenty of the half-size cards and upon these again twenty of the smallest cards. If you now fan the full-size cards, you can safely show the back of the fan since the back design of the smaller cards blends with the visible portion of the back design of the full-size cards. Arrange the cards so that the rear card of the packet of full-size cards is the same as the face card of the half-size cards, and the rear card of this latter packet is the same as the face card of the smallest packet.

EFFECT: In picking up the twenty full-size cards, take with them the two smaller packets, holding all three in the left hand, Fig. 1. With the right hand place the three packets upright, face outwards, in the left hand,

and make a fan with the full-size cards, using both hands. Show the fanned cards back and front, keeping the hand in a natural motion.

2.   Close the fan, holding the cards as in Fig. 1, and with the right hand remove all the full-size cards except the rear card which matches the face card of the half-size packet. Fan the full-size cards outwards with the right hand and move this hand over the left hand as you fan it with the spread, Fig. 2. Clip the single full-size card remaining in the left hand, between the first and second fingers of the right hand, behind the fan of cards, and carry it away,

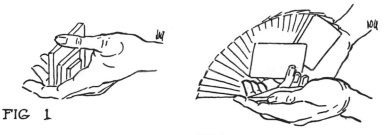

FIG 1

FIG 2

3.   Show that the cards in the left hand have shrunk to half their former size and drop the full size cards upon the table. The illusion is clinched by the fact that the face card of the packet remains the same, but it is now only half its former size.

4.   Fan the half-size cards with both hands and show them back and front, the smallest cards blending into the back design of the fan.

5.   With the right hand remove all the half-size cards save the rear card which matches the face card of the smallest packet. Fan the half size cards in the right hand and, in the act of fanning the left hand, steal the lone half-size card as in the preceding action. Show that the cards have shrunk to quarter size and drop the half size cards on the table.

6.   Fan this smallest packet with both hands and show the cards on both sides. Again remove all but one card, spread them fanwise in the right hand, and with them fan the single card remaining in the left hand. Clip this card behind the fan with the first and second fingers, in exactly the same manner as before, and, at the same time, turn the back of the left hand to the audience. Tap its back with these cards and toss them onto the table.

7.   Move the left fingers as if crumbling the cards to nothingness, open it and show it empty.

This is the only method, with packs graded in size, in which the backs and the faces can be shown at all times.

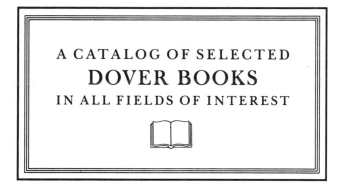

A CATALOG OF SELECTED
DOVER BOOKS
IN ALL FIELDS OF INTEREST

A CATALOG OF SELECTED DOVER
BOOKS IN ALL FIELDS OF INTEREST

DRAWINGS OF REMBRANDT, edited by Seymour Slive. Updated Lippmann, Hofstede de Groot edition, with definitive scholarly apparatus. All portraits, biblical sketches, landscapes, nudes. Oriental figures, classical studies, together with selection of work by followers. 550 illustrations. Total of 630pp. 9⅛ × 12¼.
21485-0, 21486-9 Pa., Two-vol. set $25.00

GHOST AND HORROR STORIES OF AMBROSE BIERCE, Ambrose Bierce. 24 tales vividly imagined, strangely prophetic, and decades ahead of their time in technical skill: "The Damned Thing," "An Inhabitant of Carcosa," "The Eyes of the Panther," "Moxon's Master," and 20 more. 199pp. 5⅜ × 8½. 20767-6 Pa. $3.95

ETHICAL WRITINGS OF MAIMONIDES, Maimonides. Most significant ethical works of great medieval sage, newly translated for utmost precision, readability. Laws Concerning Character Traits, Eight Chapters, more. 192pp. 5⅜ × 8½.
24522-5 Pa. $4.50

THE EXPLORATION OF THE COLORADO RIVER AND ITS CANYONS, J. W. Powell. Full text of Powell's 1,000-mile expedition down the fabled Colorado in 1869. Superb account of terrain, geology, vegetation, Indians, famine, mutiny, treacherous rapids, mighty canyons, during exploration of last unknown part of continental U.S. 400pp. 5⅜ × 8½. 20094-9 Pa. $6.95

HISTORY OF PHILOSOPHY, Julián Marías. Clearest one-volume history on the market. Every major philosopher and dozens of others, to Existentialism and later. 505pp. 5⅜ × 8½. 21739-6 Pa. $8.50

ALL ABOUT LIGHTNING, Martin A. Uman. Highly readable non-technical survey of nature and causes of lightning, thunderstorms, ball lightning, St. Elmo's Fire, much more. Illustrated. 192pp. 5⅜ × 8½. 25237-X Pa. $5.95

SAILING ALONE AROUND THE WORLD, Captain Joshua Slocum. First man to sail around the world, alone, in small boat. One of great feats of seamanship told in delightful manner. 67 illustrations. 294pp. 5⅜ × 8½. 20326-3 Pa. $4.95

LETTERS AND NOTES ON THE MANNERS, CUSTOMS AND CONDITIONS OF THE NORTH AMERICAN INDIANS, George Catlin. Classic account of life among Plains Indians: ceremonies, hunt, warfare, etc. 312 plates. 572pp. of text. 6⅛ × 9¼. 22118-0, 22119-9 Pa. Two-vol. set $15.90

ALASKA: The Harriman Expedition, 1899, John Burroughs, John Muir, et al. Informative, engrossing accounts of two-month, 9,000-mile expedition. Native peoples, wildlife, forests, geography, salmon industry, glaciers, more. Profusely illustrated. 240 black-and-white line drawings. 124 black-and-white photographs. 3 maps. Index. 576pp. 5⅜ × 8½. 25109-8 Pa. $11.95

ILLUSTRATED DICTIONARY OF HISTORIC ARCHITECTURE, edited by Cyril M. Harris. Extraordinary compendium of clear, concise definitions for over 5,000 important architectural terms complemented by over 2,000 line drawings. Covers full spectrum of architecture from ancient ruins to 20th-century Modernism. Preface. 592pp. 7½ × 9⅝. 24444-X Pa. $14.95

THE NIGHT BEFORE CHRISTMAS, Clement Moore. Full text, and woodcuts from original 1848 book. Also critical, historical material. 19 illustrations. 40pp. 4⅝ × 6. 22797-9 Pa. $2.50

THE LESSON OF JAPANESE ARCHITECTURE: 165 Photographs, Jiro Harada. Memorable gallery of 165 photographs taken in the 1930's of exquisite Japanese homes of the well-to-do and historic buildings. 13 line diagrams. 192pp. 8⅜ × 11¼. 24778-3 Pa. $8.95

THE AUTOBIOGRAPHY OF CHARLES DARWIN AND SELECTED LETTERS, edited by Francis Darwin. The fascinating life of eccentric genius composed of an intimate memoir by Darwin (intended for his children); commentary by his son, Francis; hundreds of fragments from notebooks, journals, papers; and letters to and from Lyell, Hooker, Huxley, Wallace and Henslow. xi + 365pp. 5⅜ × 8. 20479-0 Pa. $5.95

WONDERS OF THE SKY: Observing Rainbows, Comets, Eclipses, the Stars and Other Phenomena, Fred Schaaf. Charming, easy-to-read poetic guide to all manner of celestial events visible to the naked eye. Mock suns, glories, Belt of Venus, more. Illustrated. 299pp. 5¼ × 8¼. 24402-4 Pa. $7.95

BURNHAM'S CELESTIAL HANDBOOK, Robert Burnham, Jr. Thorough guide to the stars beyond our solar system. Exhaustive treatment. Alphabetical by constellation: Andromeda to Cetus in Vol. 1; Chamaeleon to Orion in Vol. 2; and Pavo to Vulpecula in Vol. 3. Hundreds of illustrations. Index in Vol. 3. 2,000pp. 6⅛ × 9¼. 23567-X, 23568-8, 23673-0 Pa., Three-vol. set $37.85

STAR NAMES: Their Lore and Meaning, Richard Hinckley Allen. Fascinating history of names various cultures have given to constellations and literary and folkloristic uses that have been made of stars. Indexes to subjects. Arabic and Greek names. Biblical references. Bibliography. 563pp. 5⅜ × 8½. 21079-0 Pa. $7.95

THIRTY YEARS THAT SHOOK PHYSICS: The Story of Quantum Theory, George Gamow. Lucid, accessible introduction to influential theory of energy and matter. Careful explanations of Dirac's anti-particles, Bohr's model of the atom, much more. 12 plates. Numerous drawings. 240pp. 5⅜ × 8½. 24895-X Pa. $4.95

CHINESE DOMESTIC FURNITURE IN PHOTOGRAPHS AND MEASURED DRAWINGS, Gustav Ecke. A rare volume, now affordably priced for antique collectors, furniture buffs and art historians. Detailed review of styles ranging from early Shang to late Ming. Unabridged republication. 161 black-and-white drawings, photos. Total of 224pp. 8⅜ × 11¼. (Available in U.S. only) 25171-3 Pa. $12.95

VINCENT VAN GOGH: A Biography, Julius Meier-Graefe. Dynamic, penetrating study of artist's life, relationship with brother, Theo, painting techniques, travels, more. Readable, engrossing. 160pp. 5⅜ × 8½. (Available in U.S. only) 25253-1 Pa. $3.95

HOW TO WRITE, Gertrude Stein. Gertrude Stein claimed anyone could understand her unconventional writing—here are clues to help. Fascinating improvisations, language experiments, explanations illuminate Stein's craft and the art of writing. Total of 414pp. 4⅜ × 6⅜. 23144-5 Pa. $5.95

ADVENTURES AT SEA IN THE GREAT AGE OF SAIL: Five Firsthand Narratives, edited by Elliot Snow. Rare true accounts of exploration, whaling, shipwreck, fierce natives, trade, shipboard life, more. 33 illustrations. Introduction. 353pp. 5⅜ × 8½. 25177-2 Pa. $7.95

THE HERBAL OR GENERAL HISTORY OF PLANTS, John Gerard. Classic descriptions of about 2,850 plants—with over 2,700 illustrations—includes Latin and English names, physical descriptions, varieties, time and place of growth, more. 2,706 illustrations. xlv + 1,678pp. 8½ × 12¼. 23147-X Cloth. $75.00

DOROTHY AND THE WIZARD IN OZ, L. Frank Baum. Dorothy and the Wizard visit the center of the Earth, where people are vegetables, glass houses grow and Oz characters reappear. Classic sequel to *Wizard of Oz*. 256pp. 5⅜ × 8. 24714-7 Pa. $4.95

SONGS OF EXPERIENCE: Facsimile Reproduction with 26 Plates in Full Color, William Blake. This facsimile of Blake's original "Illuminated Book" reproduces 26 full-color plates from a rare 1826 edition. Includes "The Tyger," "London," "Holy Thursday," and other immortal poems. 26 color plates. Printed text of poems. 48pp. 5¼ × 7. 24636-1 Pa. $3.50

SONGS OF INNOCENCE, William Blake. The first and most popular of Blake's famous "Illuminated Books," in a facsimile edition reproducing all 31 brightly colored plates. Additional printed text of each poem. 64pp. 5¼ × 7. 22764-2 Pa. $3.50

PRECIOUS STONES, Max Bauer. Classic, thorough study of diamonds, rubies, emeralds, garnets, etc.: physical character, occurrence, properties, use, similar topics. 20 plates, 8 in color. 94 figures. 659pp. 6⅛ × 9¼. 21910-0, 21911-9 Pa., Two-vol. set $15.90

ENCYCLOPEDIA OF VICTORIAN NEEDLEWORK, S. F. A. Caulfeild and Blanche Saward. Full, precise descriptions of stitches, techniques for dozens of needlecrafts—most exhaustive reference of its kind. Over 800 figures. Total of 679pp. 8⅛ × 11. Two volumes. Vol. 1 22800-2 Pa. $11.95
Vol. 2 22801-0 Pa. $11.95

THE MARVELOUS LAND OF OZ, L. Frank Baum. Second Oz book, the Scarecrow and Tin Woodman are back with hero named Tip, Oz magic. 136 illustrations. 287pp. 5⅜ × 8½. 20692-0 Pa. $5.95

WILD FOWL DECOYS, Joel Barber. Basic book on the subject, by foremost authority and collector. Reveals history of decoy making and rigging, place in American culture, different kinds of decoys, how to make them, and how to use them. 140 plates. 156pp. 7⅞ × 10¾. 20011-6 Pa. $8.95

HISTORY OF LACE, Mrs. Bury Palliser. Definitive, profusely illustrated chronicle of lace from earliest times to late 19th century. Laces of Italy, Greece, England, France, Belgium, etc. Landmark of needlework scholarship. 266 illustrations. 672pp. 6⅛ × 9¼. 24742-2 Pa. $14.95

ILLUSTRATED GUIDE TO SHAKER FURNITURE, Robert Meader. All furniture and appurtenances, with much on unknown local styles. 235 photos. 146pp. 9 × 12. 22819-3 Pa. $7.95

WHALE SHIPS AND WHALING: A Pictorial Survey, George Francis Dow. Over 200 vintage engravings, drawings, photographs of barks, brigs, cutters, other vessels. Also harpoons, lances, whaling guns, many other artifacts. Comprehensive text by foremost authority. 207 black-and-white illustrations. 288pp. 6 × 9. 24808-9 Pa. $8.95

THE BERTRAMS, Anthony Trollope. Powerful portrayal of blind self-will and thwarted ambition includes one of Trollope's most heartrending love stories. 497pp. 5⅜ × 8½. 25119-5 Pa. $8.95

ADVENTURES WITH A HAND LENS, Richard Headstrom. Clearly written guide to observing and studying flowers and grasses, fish scales, moth and insect wings, egg cases, buds, feathers, seeds, leaf scars, moss, molds, ferns, common crystals, etc.—all with an ordinary, inexpensive magnifying glass. 209 exact line drawings aid in your discoveries. 220pp. 5⅜ × 8½. 23330-8 Pa. $4.50

RODIN ON ART AND ARTISTS, Auguste Rodin. Great sculptor's candid, wide-ranging comments on meaning of art; great artists; relation of sculpture to poetry, painting, music; philosophy of life, more. 76 superb black-and-white illustrations of Rodin's sculpture, drawings and prints. 119pp. 8⅜ × 11¼. 24487-3 Pa. $6.95

FIFTY CLASSIC FRENCH FILMS, 1912–1982: A Pictorial Record, Anthony Slide. Memorable stills from Grand Illusion, Beauty and the Beast, Hiroshima, Mon Amour, many more. Credits, plot synopses, reviews, etc. 160pp. 8¼ × 11. 25256-6 Pa. $11.95

THE PRINCIPLES OF PSYCHOLOGY, William James. Famous long course complete, unabridged. Stream of thought, time perception, memory, experimental methods; great work decades ahead of its time. 94 figures. 1,391pp. 5⅜ × 8½. 20381-6, 20382-4 Pa., Two-vol. set $19.90

BODIES IN A BOOKSHOP, R. T. Campbell. Challenging mystery of blackmail and murder with ingenious plot and superbly drawn characters. In the best tradition of British suspense fiction. 192pp. 5⅜ × 8½. 24720-1 Pa. $3.95

CALLAS: PORTRAIT OF A PRIMA DONNA, George Jellinek. Renowned commentator on the musical scene chronicles incredible career and life of the most controversial, fascinating, influential operatic personality of our time. 64 black-and-white photographs. 416pp. 5⅜ × 8¼. 25047-4 Pa. $7.95

GEOMETRY, RELATIVITY AND THE FOURTH DIMENSION, Rudolph Rucker. Exposition of fourth dimension, concepts of relativity as Flatland characters continue adventures. Popular, easily followed yet accurate, profound. 141 illustrations. 133pp. 5⅜ × 8½. 23400-2 Pa. $3.50

HOUSEHOLD STORIES BY THE BROTHERS GRIMM, with pictures by Walter Crane. 53 classic stories—Rumpelstiltskin, Rapunzel, Hansel and Gretel, the Fisherman and his Wife, Snow White, Tom Thumb, Sleeping Beauty, Cinderella, and so much more—lavishly illustrated with original 19th century drawings. 114 illustrations. x + 269pp. 5⅜ × 8½. 21080-4 Pa. $4.50

CHRISTMAS CUSTOMS AND TRADITIONS, Clement A. Miles. Origin, evolution, significance of religious, secular practices. Caroling, gifts, yule logs, much more. Full, scholarly yet fascinating; non-sectarian. 400pp. 5⅜ × 8½.
23354-5 Pa. $6.50

THE HUMAN FIGURE IN MOTION, Eadweard Muybridge. More than 4,500 stopped-action photos, in action series, showing undraped men, women, children jumping, lying down, throwing, sitting, wrestling, carrying, etc. 390pp. 7⅞ × 10⅝.
20204-6 Cloth. $19.95

THE MAN WHO WAS THURSDAY, Gilbert Keith Chesterton. Witty, fast-paced novel about a club of anarchists in turn-of-the-century London. Brilliant social, religious, philosophical speculations. 128pp. 5⅜ × 8½. 25121-7 Pa. $3.95

A CEZANNE SKETCHBOOK: Figures, Portraits, Landscapes and Still Lifes, Paul Cezanne. Great artist experiments with tonal effects, light, mass, other qualities in over 100 drawings. A revealing view of developing master painter, precursor of Cubism. 102 black-and-white illustrations. 144pp. 8¾ × 6⅜. 24790-2 Pa. $5.95

AN ENCYCLOPEDIA OF BATTLES: Accounts of Over 1,560 Battles from 1479 B.C. to the Present, David Eggenberger. Presents essential details of every major battle in recorded history, from the first battle of Megiddo in 1479 B.C. to Grenada in 1984. List of Battle Maps. New Appendix covering the years 1967–1984. Index. 99 illustrations. 544pp. 6½ × 9¼. 24913-1 Pa. $14.95

AN ETYMOLOGICAL DICTIONARY OF MODERN ENGLISH, Ernest Weekley. Richest, fullest work, by foremost British lexicographer. Detailed word histories. Inexhaustible. Total of 856pp. 6½ × 9¼.
21873-2, 21874-0 Pa., Two-vol. set $17.00

WEBSTER'S AMERICAN MILITARY BIOGRAPHIES, edited by Robert McHenry. Over 1,000 figures who shaped 3 centuries of American military history. Detailed biographies of Nathan Hale, Douglas MacArthur, Mary Hallaren, others. Chronologies of engagements, more. Introduction. Addenda. 1,033 entries in alphabetical order. xi + 548pp. 6½ × 9¼. (Available in U.S. only)
24758-9 Pa. $11.95

LIFE IN ANCIENT EGYPT, Adolf Erman. Detailed older account, with much not in more recent books: domestic life, religion, magic, medicine, commerce, and whatever else needed for complete picture. Many illustrations. 597pp. 5⅜ × 8½.
22632-8 Pa. $8.95

HISTORIC COSTUME IN PICTURES, Braun & Schneider. Over 1,450 costumed figures shown, covering a wide variety of peoples: kings, emperors, nobles, priests, servants, soldiers, scholars, townsfolk, peasants, merchants, courtiers, cavaliers, and more. 256pp. 8⅜ × 11¼. 23150-X Pa. $7.95

THE NOTEBOOKS OF LEONARDO DA VINCI, edited by J. P. Richter. Extracts from manuscripts reveal great genius; on painting, sculpture, anatomy, sciences, geography, etc. Both Italian and English. 186 ms. pages reproduced, plus 500 additional drawings, including studies for *Last Supper, Sforza* monument, etc. 860pp. 7⅞ × 10¾. (Available in U.S. only) 22572-0, 22573-9 Pa., Two-vol. set $25.90

THE ART NOUVEAU STYLE BOOK OF ALPHONSE MUCHA: All 72 Plates from "Documents Decoratifs" in Original Color, Alphonse Mucha. Rare copyright-free design portfolio by high priest of Art Nouveau. Jewelry, wallpaper, stained glass, furniture, figure studies, plant and animal motifs, etc. Only complete one-volume edition. 80pp. 9⅜ × 12¼. 24044-4 Pa. $8.95

ANIMALS: 1,419 COPYRIGHT-FREE ILLUSTRATIONS OF MAMMALS, BIRDS, FISH, INSECTS, ETC., edited by Jim Harter. Clear wood engravings present, in extremely lifelike poses, over 1,000 species of animals. One of the most extensive pictorial sourcebooks of its kind. Captions. Index. 284pp. 9 × 12. 23766-4 Pa. $9.95

OBELISTS FLY HIGH, C. Daly King. Masterpiece of American detective fiction, long out of print, involves murder on a 1935 transcontinental flight—"a very thrilling story"—NY Times. Unabridged and unaltered republication of the edition published by William Collins Sons & Co. Ltd., London, 1935. 288pp. 5⅜ × 8½. (Available in U.S. only) 25036-9 Pa. $4.95

VICTORIAN AND EDWARDIAN FASHION: A Photographic Survey, Alison Gernsheim. First fashion history completely illustrated by contemporary photographs. Full text plus 235 photos, 1840–1914, in which many celebrities appear. 240pp. 6½ × 9¼. 24205-6 Pa. $6.00

THE ART OF THE FRENCH ILLUSTRATED BOOK, 1700–1914, Gordon N. Ray. Over 630 superb book illustrations by Fragonard, Delacroix, Daumier, Doré, Grandville, Manet, Mucha, Steinlen, Toulouse-Lautrec and many others. Preface. Introduction. 633 halftones. Indices of artists, authors & titles, binders and provenances. Appendices. Bibliography. 608pp. 8⅜ × 11¼. 25086-5 Pa. $24.95

THE WONDERFUL WIZARD OF OZ, L. Frank Baum. Facsimile in full color of America's finest children's classic. 143 illustrations by W. W. Denslow. 267pp. 5⅜ × 8½. 20691-2 Pa. $5.95

FRONTIERS OF MODERN PHYSICS: New Perspectives on Cosmology, Relativity, Black Holes and Extraterrestrial Intelligence, Tony Rothman, et al. For the intelligent layman. Subjects include: cosmological models of the universe; black holes; the neutrino; the search for extraterrestrial intelligence. Introduction. 46 black-and-white illustrations. 192pp. 5⅜ × 8½. 24587-X Pa. $6.95

THE FRIENDLY STARS, Martha Evans Martin & Donald Howard Menzel. Classic text marshalls the stars together in an engaging, non-technical survey, presenting them as sources of beauty in night sky. 23 illustrations. Foreword. 2 star charts. Index. 147pp. 5⅜ × 8½. 21099-5 Pa. $3.50

FADS AND FALLACIES IN THE NAME OF SCIENCE, Martin Gardner. Fair, witty appraisal of cranks, quacks, and quackeries of science and pseudoscience: hollow earth, Velikovsky, orgone energy, Dianetics, flying saucers, Bridey Murphy, food and medical fads, etc. Revised, expanded In the Name of Science. "A very able and even-tempered presentation."—The New Yorker. 363pp. 5⅜ × 8. 20394-8 Pa. $6.50

ANCIENT EGYPT: ITS CULTURE AND HISTORY, J. E Manchip White. From pre-dynastics through Ptolemies: society, history, political structure, religion, daily life, literature, cultural heritage. 48 plates. 217pp. 5⅜ × 8½. 22548-8 Pa. $4.95

SIR HARRY HOTSPUR OF HUMBLETHWAITE, Anthony Trollope. Incisive, unconventional psychological study of a conflict between a wealthy baronet, his idealistic daughter, and their scapegrace cousin. The 1870 novel in its first inexpensive edition in years. 250pp. 5⅜ × 8½. 24953-0 Pa. $5.95

LASERS AND HOLOGRAPHY, Winston E. Kock. Sound introduction to burgeoning field, expanded (1981) for second edition. Wave patterns, coherence, lasers, diffraction, zone plates, properties of holograms, recent advances. 84 illustrations. 160pp. 5⅜ × 8¼. (Except in United Kingdom) 24041-X Pa. $3.50

INTRODUCTION TO ARTIFICIAL INTELLIGENCE: SECOND, ENLARGED EDITION, Philip C. Jackson, Jr. Comprehensive survey of artificial intelligence—the study of how machines (computers) can be made to act intelligently. Includes introductory and advanced material. Extensive notes updating the main text. 132 black-and-white illustrations. 512pp. 5⅜ × 8½. 24864-X Pa. $8.95

HISTORY OF INDIAN AND INDONESIAN ART, Ananda K. Coomaraswamy. Over 400 illustrations illuminate classic study of Indian art from earliest Harappa finds to early 20th century. Provides philosophical, religious and social insights. 304pp. 6⅜ × 9⅜. 25005-9 Pa. $8.95

THE GOLEM, Gustav Meyrink. Most famous supernatural novel in modern European literature, set in Ghetto of Old Prague around 1890. Compelling story of mystical experiences, strange transformations, profound terror. 13 black-and-white illustrations. 224pp. 5⅜ × 8½. (Available in U.S. only) 25025-3 Pa. $5.95

ARMADALE, Wilkie Collins. Third great mystery novel by the author of *The Woman in White* and *The Moonstone*. Original magazine version with 40 illustrations. 597pp. 5⅜ × 8½. 23429-0 Pa. $9.95

PICTORIAL ENCYCLOPEDIA OF HISTORIC ARCHITECTURAL PLANS, DETAILS AND ELEMENTS: With 1,880 Line Drawings of Arches, Domes, Doorways, Facades, Gables, Windows, etc., John Theodore Haneman. Sourcebook of inspiration for architects, designers, others. Bibliography. Captions. 141pp. 9 × 12. 24605-1 Pa. $6.95

BENCHLEY LOST AND FOUND, Robert Benchley. Finest humor from early 30's, about pet peeves, child psychologists, post office and others. Mostly unavailable elsewhere. 73 illustrations by Peter Arno and others. 183pp. 5⅜ × 8½. 22410-4 Pa. $3.95

ERTÉ GRAPHICS, Erté. Collection of striking color graphics: *Seasons, Alphabet, Numerals, Aces* and *Precious Stones*. 50 plates, including 4 on covers. 48pp. 9⅜ × 12¼. 23580-7 Pa. $6.95

THE JOURNAL OF HENRY D. THOREAU, edited by Bradford Torrey, F. H. Allen. Complete reprinting of 14 volumes, 1837–61, over two million words; the sourcebooks for *Walden*, etc. Definitive. All original sketches, plus 75 photographs. 1,804pp. 8½ × 12¼. 20312-3, 20313-1 Cloth., Two-vol. set $80.00

CASTLES: THEIR CONSTRUCTION AND HISTORY, Sidney Toy. Traces castle development from ancient roots. Nearly 200 photographs and drawings illustrate moats, keeps, baileys, many other features. Caernarvon, Dover Castles, Hadrian's Wall, Tower of London, dozens more. 256pp. 5⅜ × 8¼. 24898-4 Pa. $5.95

AMERICAN CLIPPER SHIPS: 1833–1858, Octavius T. Howe & Frederick C. Matthews. Fully-illustrated, encyclopedic review of 352 clipper ships from the period of America's greatest maritime supremacy. Introduction. 109 halftones. 5 black-and-white line illustrations. Index. Total of 928pp. 5⅜ × 8½.
25115-2, 25116-0 Pa., Two-vol. set $17.90

TOWARDS A NEW ARCHITECTURE, Le Corbusier. Pioneering manifesto by great architect, near legendary founder of "International School." Technical and aesthetic theories, views on industry, economics, relation of form to function, "mass-production spirit," much more. Profusely illustrated. Unabridged translation of 13th French edition. Introduction by Frederick Etchells. 320pp. 6⅛ × 9¼. (Available in U.S. only) 25023-7 Pa. $8.95

THE BOOK OF KELLS, edited by Blanche Cirker. Inexpensive collection of 32 full-color, full-page plates from the greatest illuminated manuscript of the Middle Ages, painstakingly reproduced from rare facsimile edition. Publisher's Note. Captions. 32pp. 9⅜ × 12¼. 24345-1 Pa. $4.95

BEST SCIENCE FICTION STORIES OF H. G. WELLS, H. G. Wells. Full novel *The Invisible Man*, plus 17 short stories: "The Crystal Egg," "Aepyornis Island," "The Strange Orchid," etc. 303pp. 5⅜ × 8½. (Available in U.S. only)
21531-8 Pa. $4.95

AMERICAN SAILING SHIPS: Their Plans and History, Charles G. Davis. Photos, construction details of schooners, frigates, clippers, other sailcraft of 18th to early 20th centuries—plus entertaining discourse on design, rigging, nautical lore, much more. 137 black-and-white illustrations. 240pp. 6⅛ × 9¼.
24658-2 Pa. $5.95

ENTERTAINING MATHEMATICAL PUZZLES, Martin Gardner. Selection of author's favorite conundrums involving arithmetic, money, speed, etc., with lively commentary. Complete solutions. 112pp. 5⅜ × 8½. 25211-6 Pa. $2.95

THE WILL TO BELIEVE, HUMAN IMMORTALITY, William James. Two books bound together. Effect of irrational on logical, and arguments for human immortality. 402pp. 5⅜ × 8½. 20291-7 Pa. $7.50

THE HAUNTED MONASTERY and THE CHINESE MAZE MURDERS, Robert Van Gulik. 2 full novels by Van Gulik continue adventures of Judge Dee and his companions. An evil Taoist monastery, seemingly supernatural events; overgrown topiary maze that hides strange crimes. Set in 7th-century China. 27 illustrations. 328pp. 5⅜ × 8½. 23502-5 Pa. $5.95

CELEBRATED CASES OF JUDGE DEE (DEE GOONG AN), translated by Robert Van Gulik. Authentic 18th-century Chinese detective novel; Dee and associates solve three interlocked cases. Led to Van Gulik's own stories with same characters. Extensive introduction. 9 illustrations. 237pp. 5⅜ × 8½.
23337-5 Pa. $4.95

Prices subject to change without notice.
Available at your book dealer or write for free catalog to Dept. GI, Dover Publications, Inc., 31 East 2nd St., Mineola, N.Y. 11501. Dover publishes more than 175 books each year on science, elementary and advanced mathematics, biology, music, art, literary history, social sciences and other areas.